# CHILD LABOUR: FROM PERU TO PHILIPPINES

JASHANDEEP SINGH KANG

Dedicated to my maternal grandftaher Balour Singh Brar and paternal grandfather Swaran Singh Kang.

# Contents

# Contents

# FOREWORD

"Where the mind is without fear and the head is held high
Where knowledge is free
Where the world has not been broken up into fragments
By narrow domestic walls
Where words come out from the depth of truth
Where tireless striving stretches its arms towards perfection
Where the clear stream of reason has not lost its way
Into the dreary desert sand of dead habit
Where the mind is led forward by thee
Into ever-widening thought and action
Into that heaven of freedom, my Father, let my country awake."
-Rabindranath Tagore

# I

# GHOST OF CHE GUEVARA: BOLIVIAN MINES

Date: 9 October, 1967; Place: La Higuera, Bolivia.

A school with substandard infrastructure was heavily guarded by the Bolivian army because a famous revolutionary was recently captured from the jungle and was imprisoned in one of its rooms. It was the same person who had given a thunderous speech in the United Nations General Assembly, a few years ago and had received a standing ovation from the representatives of other nations.

The Captain of Bolivian Army looked at his worn-out clothes, his dusty hair and he recalled seeing his images in the newspapers, standing next to Mao Zedong, Pt. Nehru, and other eminent politicians of the world (that too in blazer and boots). He asked him why he didn't surrender when the Bolivian government had already taken up socialist reforms. "And after surrender, *where would I go then..?*" he replied. But as fate would have it, President of Bolivia Rene Barrientos, then approved his execution. Subsequently, a half-drunk, 27- year-old sergeant, Mario Teran entered the schoolroom and 9 bullet shots were heard by the people outside. It was the end of a controversial yet famous Cuban revolutionary (and Cuban minister) named Che Guevara. His hands were chopped off and sent back to Fidel Castro, and his body was secretly buried somewhere in Bolivia. No doubt his reply to the Captain of the Bolivian Army had some deeper historic connotations but his statement deserves attention in a sense that sometimes you continue because you have nowhere to go! Because, you have no place to go! The same is true with the numerous child laborers today.

Che was an Argentine doctor but during his motorcycle journey to Latin America, he was moved by horrible realities of the mines, he saw the children as young as 6 working there in inhumane conditions. Decades after his death, Bolivian mines still present an abysmal situation.

Santiago and Augustine are aged 12 and 14 years respectively. They live near the silver mines with their mother and two sisters. Their father was a miner in the same mine. He had died a few years back because of a lung disease. Still, the two boys risk their lives in the rat-hole tunnels, which are acutely dangerous and claustrophobic. They labour hard and earn 2-3 Tors per day but are able to purchase bread for the family. They often take cigars and some alcohol deep down into the tunnels as a gift to the shrine of Uncle Takitachito, who protects them during their mining expeditions. They spend their day, hammering the rock and pushing the heavy trolleys amidst the persistent risk of collapse of the tunnel. One such accident had recently consumed the life of a laborer, who was of their age. Though there is an oxygen supply it is still difficult to breathe in these tunnels. Every day the dust chokes the bronchioles of their lungs yet they have never heard about the disease Silicosis. In summation they do it for survival; that is life all about!

Nearby there is a hill of Cerro Rico which is referred to as the hill that eats men. Mining had begun 500 years ago and since then 4 lakh men have lost their lives. Jose Luis is working there since the age of 12. His father doesn't earn enough money for the survival of the family, therefore he has to work. He wants to study and doesn't like mining at all. "People are dying and minerals are drying but my job provides fast cash. Kids here make 10 times more than a street flower seller", he says.

A few hundred kilometers away, lives a boy called Alfredo who is 16. He works as a clown to entertain children. He had started working as a bus announcer when he was 8. Nearby, there is another child named David Mamani whose employer had not paid him for the last 6 months. David says that there also exists a brutal world where you will not find the fun and joy seen on the swings of Disneyland.

Not far away is the city of Potosi, where a boy named Juan Carlos aged 13, cleans tombstones in the Sucre cemetery. He places flowers on the tombs and gets paid by the family members. His mother had died when he was 9 and he works in the cemetery with his younger sister. He dreams to become a lawyer. His elder brother had died a few years ago due to over use of drugs but his life is too busy to visit his brother's tombstone in a different cemetery.

In the same city is a union of 15000 Child and Adolescent workers called Unatsbo. They are lobbying to lower the minimum age of employment below 14. The members say, "Child labour cannot be eradicated without providing alternatives or social security. It is a harsh reality, and outlawing child labor will only lead to poorer working conditions. There is a need to regulate our jobs so that kids have the same rights as adults, at the workplaces."

**Philosophical underline**

The only issue with these kids is that "*They don't know anything different*". It is what their parents did; it is what their friends do and therefore it is totally fine for them. They just don't know that they are suffering. Let's understand it like this, if a newborn baby is poked with a sharp object, it may not cause serious harm but there is pain. These child laborers are poked throughout their lives. They feel pain but that is all they have always known; it is their way of living. They don't know anything else. If someone doesn't know anything different, doesn't mean that they don't suffer.

# II

# PERU: THE MERCURY FUMES

Up a cloud forest trail in south East Peru, lays the famous Machu Picchu, a royal retreat built for the Inca emperor. It clings to a mountain spur 8000 feet up in the Andes. This is an insignia of the Inca Empire, an empire that had expanded in the $15^{th}$ century. But apart from the gloss and shine of the empire, there was a dark side to it and that was child labour and child sacrifices, which had existed since the glorious Mayan civilization of Latin America. While the practice of child sacrifice gradually declined, child labour persisted after Peru's independence in 1824, (following the Spanish-American wars of independence led by San Jose Martin and Bolivar).

Peru is now the largest gold producer in Latin America. It produces nearly 15 tonnes of gold every year. Nearly 50000 children in Peru grind the ore in an old-fashioned way and children as young as six, work in the gold mines. A child labourer says, "Everybody tells us not to work and to go to school but nobody helps us. I have brothers and sisters to feed."Children work for 7-8 hours and bear the risk of tunnel collapse. Moreover, during the process of purification of gold, they handle Mercury as if the kid is handling a juicy candy. They are hardly aware about the adverse effects of mercury on their nervous system. And what else, it becomes worse during the heating of Gold-Mercury amalgam; they sit without protective gears and hence inhale the toxic fumes of Mercury which may cause Minamata disease and subsequent loss of sensation in feet, hearing impairment etc. Maybe one doesn't care about long-term health effects when one is worried about the daily survival. Their vision becomes parochial and their scope of thinking is narrowed down. Probably that is the very fate of 3 million children, aged between 5 to17 in Peru.

No doubt there have been efforts like 450 students were rescued in Central Philimina by an NGO called Coparixion in association with ILO. Coparixion and other local NGOs had also facilitated the formation of a miners association that has set up an ore processing plant, which has further created jobs for the local adults.

Similarly, numerous children are working as sellers, vendors, cleaners, and maids in cities like Lima. Moreover, just like Bolivia, there is also a child labour union in Peru called Mantok. Apart from protecting the rights of working children, it is also trying to ensure basic schooling for these workers.

**Philosophical underline** :

When the members of Mantok say that, "we want to work", they don't mean what they say. They are saying that they want food for their family, a good shelter, etc. They want the 7 necessities of humans. They want to survive and want their families to survive. Every child deserves the joys of childhood and the opportunity to learn (that is a part of the long human rights list). If these child workers know about the joyful lives of other children, of their age, why would they love to work or why would they want to work? It is just that they have to work because somewhere the governments of the day fail to provide social security and opportunities to the vulnerable families.

# III

# BRAZIL: THE GARBAGE DUMPS

Very little was known of Brazil before the arrival of the Portuguese fleet under the command of Pedro Alvares Cabral. From the $16^{th}$-century sugarcane plantations along the northeast coast became an important part of the country's economy. The Portuguese tried to use native indigenous people (including children) as slaves to produce sugar for Europe but in the end, they resorted to bringing in slaves from Africa. Gold was discovered in Brazil at the beginning of the $18^{th}$ century resulting in a huge influx of European immigrants. The region known as Minas Gerais became the center of Brazil's gold mining and slaves including child labour were deployed. Deposits of diamonds were also discovered in 1729 in the region now known as Diamantine. Portuguese ruled this vast empire from Rio De Janerio. But following the war of Independence, Brazil ceased to be a Portuguese colony in 1822 and finally, it became a republic in 1889. Even after becoming a republic, the issue of child labour persisted and presently 7 million children continue to work despite law banning child labour.

Somewhere in the North-East Brazil, lives a 13-year-old girl named Leandres. She lives with her mother in a single room and they cook on the bathroom floor. Her day starts with her visit to Olinda dump where garbage trucks bring the fresh garbage from the nearby cities. In the polluted, stinky, and dangerous environment she looks for cans and bottles in the garbage, 10 hours a day and all seven days a week. Whenever a garbage truck from a famous supermarket comes, there is a scramble and tough competition amongst the children for every single penny and sometimes they even get hurt. Last week, the friend of Leandres had fallen off from the truck and had to be admitted in the hospital. Once a kid was pricked with a disposed of needle and subsequently, he caught a bacterial infection. Leandre's mother Marcia sells the cans to a middleman, who further sells them for good profits. And that is how food is kept on the table. All these years Leandres has become quiet and withdrawn.

In the nearby town, resides a 33-year-old woman, named Alexandria who is training to be a nurse. At 10 she was given to another family as a maid. She says, "As a child, I missed the childhood play and I would often go to a market called Ceisa, to find vegetables and fruits from the garbage, which I would collect and to give to my family." She starts crying while telling this.

Nearby is the town of Sao Paulo, where working young is culturally acceptable. Children can be seen selling products on the streets. Similarly, in the state of Alagoas, a school has 1200 registered students but as the teacher quotes, a third of them don't attend the classes because they prefer selling kebabs and ice creams on the streets. Not only this, social clubs of the elderly are happy to admit that they have children working in their houses and estates as they consider child labour as a form of social service.

**Philosophical underline**

Childhood is the phase during which, spreading the severities of mature life, a person barely takes on any type of accountability or commitments. Yet, at that point, it is also true that those kids are vulnerable and susceptible. The inescapable and obstinate difficulty of child labor signifies one amongst the many majorly critical challenges of human rights, during the present era. It repudiates, kids across the globe of their essential rights to edification, playing, and wellbeing. The point that kids have a high vulnerability is why they are required to be taken care of and sheltered from the harshness of the world outside and throughout.

# IV

# ARGENTINA: CHOICE BETWEEN BOOK AND BRICK

City: Cordova

There is pin-drop silence in the class as the teacher is reciting the interesting story of a girl named Cinderella, probably the most famous story of child labour in the world. But some students are missing from the class as they are working in the nearby Brick kiln. Such a scenario is not new in Argentina, a nation that has traversed a long course of history.

Child labour had existed in the tribes inhabiting Argentina. Subsequently, it became a Spanish colony called the Vice Royalty of the Rio de la Plata. Thereafter, commercialization of agriculture gained strength. Juan Peron had taken a few steps to regulate Child labour via various government programs but the efforts were not much successful. The situation of the economy worsened after 1954 due to isolationism. Gradually the issue of Child labour became more intense.

Presently, children are involved in all kinds of labour despite all the bans. But let us take the examples of brick kilns only. There are numerous unregulated Brick factories in Cordova and regions around it. Not only locals but Bolivian migrants also work extensively in brick kilns under poor conditions. The choice between brick and a book is not a fair one for some children as it is a matter of survival for them and their families. Employers know very well that if they are caught, they may be jailed but still they employ children. On being asked as to why they do so. The reply is that they have to pay a lot as rent (somewhere around 25% of total production value), hence there is pressure to increase production and reduce wages. The result is that child labour is extensive in these brick kilns. But the question is why children? They are easy to control; can be paid less; will not unionize; may work overtime without much criticism. Hence these employers are even ready to take the risk of getting arrested. Similar is the case with Tobacco fields in Salta, South Argentina. Numerous children work on the fields; in curing centers and associated activities like drying the tobacco leaves, hand dropping the tobacco leaves over the processing belts.

In a nutshell, two things are facilitating the persistence of child labour: "Culture of employing child labour" and "Need: of both destitute families and employers"

**Philosophical underline**

Every person or child haves the right to be valued and respected for their own sake and to be treated ethically. Human Rights and basic liberties aid us in developing our inherent abilities, intellect, talents, and morality for fulfilling our substantial and psychic requirements. To completely develop as individuals, exercising and enjoying Human Rights by every individual is essential. It is unnecessary to affirm that devoid of the acknowledgment of the right towards edification, understanding of the right for developing each person as well as country is impossible. Childhood and children around the globe have largely been interpreted with regards to a 'golden age' which is equal to virtuousness, liberty, happiness, and play. Child labor is an insignia of disgust and is a demise of this golden age.

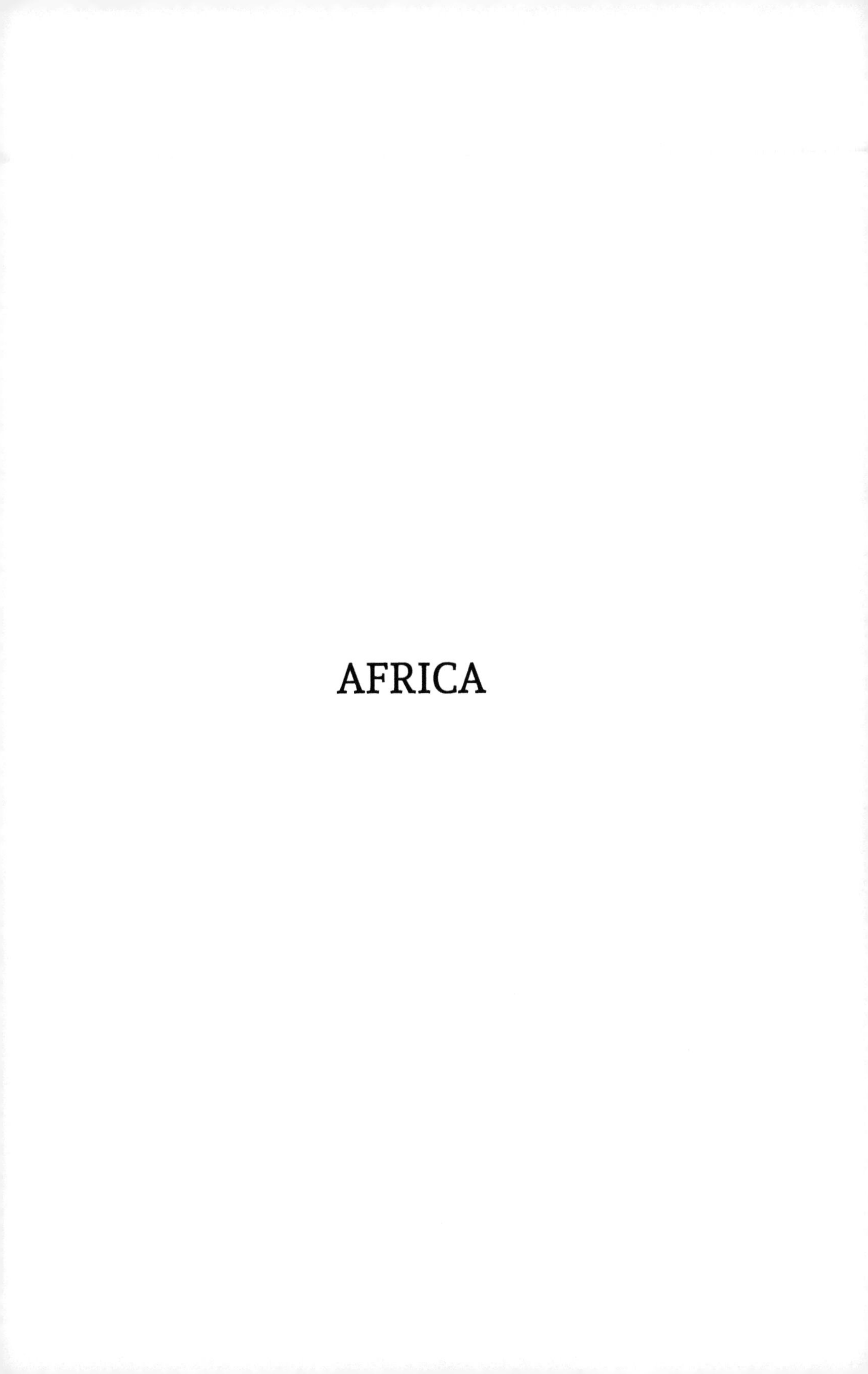

# AFRICA

# V

# YOUR SMARTPHONES!!: THE CONGOLESE MINES

Date: 17 January 1961

Place: Elisabethville, State of Katanga(Congo)

After getting beaten by the Belgian authorities, Patrice Lumumba, the First Prime minister of the independent Democratic Republic of Congo, was driven to an isolated spot where three firing squads had been assembled and were commanded by the Belgian contract officer Julien Gat. Katangan authorities were involved too. Lumumba and his two colleagues were lined up against the tree and were shot dead. His body was dismembered and dissolved in sulphuric acid to eliminate the traces of the widely popular P.M. who was to become a legend later on.

Apart from the many disputes, he had with the West, Lumumba was highly critical of the neo-imperialism and ultra commercial interests of Belgium and other nations in the mines of Katanga province. This was not only robbing the country of its wealth but was causing inhumane conditions in mines; was giving rise to the issues like child labour, of which Lumumba was highly critical.

But decades after Congo's independence, the situation of mines is still not good. The conditions of child laborers in Dikulushi silver mines are no less than modern-day slaves. They work with rudimentary tools and that too under harsh conditions. For them, cobalt and silver are as precious as gold because there is a rising demand by smartphone and laptop manufacturers.

Here an 8-year-old malnourished kid has not eaten for the last two days but is still mining in the deep tunnels. He complains that they are beaten and abused by the supervisor. "When I wake up in the morning, it scares me for I have to come here again", he says. There is a persistent danger of collapse of tunnels during rains and recently few workers had even lost their lives. There is no rope to descend into the pits, rather holes are carved on the sides of pits and the miners climb down using these holes as handles. Nobody uses masks. Similarly there is another boy, Mukumba who is 12 years old and he digs the rocks with his own hands. On being asked why he works, he replies, "Hunger is a powerful motivator".

Similarly, there is a person who works deep into the tunnels while his two sons help him on the surface. They empty the soil from bags, which are as heavy as them. One of them is a young boy named Dorsen. He has never seen an electric fan; has never seen water coming out of the tap. His life is all about helping his father for the survival of his family. On being asked about his work, he says, "Every morning we go to find a job and if they give us money we buy flour and we make Fufu and we eat." Not only this, Malian minors also work in these mines as they are brought here by the traffickers. Child slave trade exists in some or other form in the region and out of Child laborers working in Congo, 20,000 are from Mali. These children work their fingers to the bones and expose themselves to all manners of poison. Their frail bodies fit easily into the thin tunnels and as they say, their work is the only way to survive. These children get paid a pittance i.e. nearly 1 dollar every day. Zicky Suzi, a child minor says that he feels very bad because his friends go to school and he has to work in the mines. In summation, while others think of their "tomorrow", these child laborers think or are forced to think of "today".

Moreover, these boys may never own a Smartphone in their lives but their labour does forms a part of the supply chain of its components. Chinese contractors are present in the region and they are not concerned as to who digs the cobalt for them. All they look for is profit as they have to supply cobalt to a famous battery manufacturer.

Further rains usually drain away, the toxic chemicals from the mines into the only river of the region, which is the only source of water supply for people. Nearby, a fisherman points to the dead fish floating on water. Numerous people have also reported tumors and cancer, and the reason is not difficult to understand.

Films like "Blood Diamond", have sensitized people as to how we unknowingly create demand for exploitation and bloodshed, but it is just not limited to diamonds, there are numerous products around us, whose supply chain may involve the sweat of little hands; the labour of kids who have lost their youth; the labour of kids who have lost their dreams; the labour of malnourished kids who do all this for food.

**Philosophical underline**

Modern time is often said to be the testing times of extreme materialism, wrenching changes, and contradictions. It is wielding psychological and physical pressures leading us to delusions, physical sufferings, and mental agonies. Children are the utmost reward for humankind. Abandoning children suggests damage to humanity altogether. Each type of job, even if dangerous or not, involves a certain level of strain. A dangerous job has a crippling effect on a child's well-being, spirit, and character, whereas a non-dangerous job implies different types of deficit, like renunciation of admission to edification and renunciation of the enjoyable actions related to childhood. A viewpoint of human rights is essential to fully understand child labour, since it puts focus on elimination and discrimination as causative influences.

# VI

# BURKINA FASO: WHERE THE MIND IS WITHOUT FEAR

**Place**: Gold mine in Angeora, Burkina Faso.

Local radio is playing the poem of Rabindranath Tagore.

Amli and Sudan are working in the gold mines. Like always they are scared of the mine collapse but still, they lower their heads and they drag their malnourished bodies into the rat-hole tunnels.

**Radio near the mine says, "Where the Mind is without fear and the head is held high"**

On being asked as to why they don't go to school. They reply, "We don't have enough money to purchase the books and we have to support our family too."

**Radio speaks, "Where Knowledge is free."**

If the mine is looked at closely, it is organized like a mining town, which has some shops that provide for daily necessities. Adult miners have grown up in this mining town and this is the only world they have ever known.

**Radio speaks, "Where the world is not divided into fragments by narrow domestic walls."**

The poem ends with, "Into that heaven of freedom my father let my country awake". Tagore might have written this poem for his nation India, but his words are relevant for every single nation across the world.

Burkina Faso is the fourth biggest gold producer in Africa with nearly 600 mines (both industrial and traditional). Nearly 1 million people are digging for gold but still, it is one of the poorest countries in the world. Miners are like animals and savage soldiers who frantically look for their survival, feets below the ground. Many French people are looking for gold too in this region. And all this has created what is now known as the "Gold Rush of Burkina Faso".

Gold wells are nearly 10-15 meters deep and it is usually found in Quartz. 10-15 bags of white ore yield nearly 1 gram of gold. Children are involved too who play numerous roles like turning over the soil, filtering the ore, etc. Malnourished children easily go down into the holes where the temperature reaches 50 degrees Celsius. During the rainy season, tunnels are flooded with water but the work never stops. To fight fear, children consume drugs like cocaine, cannabis, and a locally available tablet. As shown earlier, when the issue is of immediate survival they do not consider long-term effects on their health. They think of today rather than tomorrow. Hence many of them are drug addicts. It is quite ironic to see the photo of Che Guevara on their T-shirts, a man who was a strong critic of children working in mines. Families make, over 1 Euro per day and while the meat is a luxury, they purchase rice and some vegetables to fill their stomachs partially, if not fully.

While UN troops were fighting a local terrorist organization in 2003, gold mine of Alkeida suddenly emerged from the sand (in a region swept by hot Harmattan winds), and therefore rush for the gold began. Now 5000 people reside in the mining town and many children work in this mine, who push heavy trawlers, work in tunnels and purify gold.

Agriculture is a risky venture, as droughts usually destroy the maize and other crops grown locally. And as far as the hazards of gold are concerned, they are quite similar to the ones seen in the case of Peru. Mercury is used with bare hands and it is mixed with the ore. It compresses the gold and finally, the amalgam is burnt without any protective gears. Hence highly toxic fumes are inhaled by children sitting nearby who don't have a pint of knowledge as to how dangerous these fumes are. Moreover, Mercury and cyanide contaminate the air and waters of the river, on which the localities depend.

Nearby is the shop of Rasmane, a gold buyer who purchases 1500 Euro worth of gold per day. He has software on his mobile, which keeps him connected with the international prices of gold. Hence payments to miners are adjusted, accordingly. He weighs the gold nugget on a balance against a match stick. He is respected by the local miners because he gives them money in advance, to purchase food and daily necessities until they find gold. He goes to a nearby market on a motorbike to sell gold to the further suppliers and he risks the infestations of Highway gangs.

The average life expectancy of a miner is 45. Lung diseases are widespread and the local doctor treats nearly 50 miners every day. Recently a 16-year-old miner was stuck in the 15-meter deep hole and he died because of suffocation. In the last two months, 4 children have died. But the most horrible incident is still fresh in the minds of miners that took place at Gombogimbiro where a strong explosion occurred in the chemical cartons (used to treat gold). 59 people were consumed by it. Nevertheless 1.5 million are employed and the gold mine industry is now a multi-billion dollars industry in Burkina Faso.

**Philosophical underline**

Destitution as well as loss of earnings influences the socio emotive environment of the household that sequentially impacts children's psychosomatic health and activities. Researches of poverty-stricken households and relations that encounter huge decreases in profits specify that the influences on children are arbitrated chiefly by the psychosomatic anguish of parents. Strategy investigators not just argue the level of good that could arise out of increasing earnings of poor families; few contend that wellbeing earnings have injurious influences too.

# VII

# THE DARK SIDE OF CHOCOLATE

“Hopeful eyes, happy smiles
Soft hands, million dreams
Is this not the identity of a child?
Then why do I see
Tear filled eyes, terrified faces
Rough hands and shattered dreams”
- Tanushree Sharma

Three million tonnes of chocolate are consumed every year and out of that half is just consumed by the Europeans alone. Chocolate brings a spark in the eyes of kids and joy in their souls. If you visit the European malls, you may find chocolates kept in luxurious, well-lit transparent cabins with some chocolate boxes as costly as 100 Euros. But the manager sitting on the counter who collects the cash would hardly know the ground realities from where the cocoa of these chocolates is procured. The truth is harsh, but it might happen that when you purchase chocolate from some brands, you may unknowingly create a demand for child labour. Shocked!! Let’s have a look at this case study.

Ivory Coast and Ghana are the biggest producers of Cocoa. No doubt, in 2001 Harkin Engel Protocol (or the Cocoa protocol) was signed by eminent companies, whereby the principle of “responsible procurement” was agreed but even years after this agreement, the ground realities are still dismal. A Swiss company is the largest supplier of mass for the cocoa industry in Europe and it procures its cocoa from Ivory Coast. Investigators took the onus to find out the ground realities. It was found that many children from Mali were smuggled into Ivory Coast from a bus station in Zegoua, South Mali. The bus carried them near the border and from there the kids were smuggled through motorcycles via a back road, in the region which is not well guarded by the security forces. Kids are smuggled not only from Mali but also from Niger and Burkina Faso. Once they cross the border, children are brought to a market, where the kids are sold to the farmers.

As per a few reports, nearly 130 children were smuggled from Zegoua, in the months preceding this investigation. Not only this, the traffickers are also financed by some plantation owners in Ivory Coast. The investigators were afraid while enquiring about ground facts because In April 2004, a French Canadian journalist Guy Andre Kieffer was kidnapped in Ivory Coast and he was never heard of again.

Ivory Coast alone accounts for 42% of Cocoa produced in Africa. In Abidjan, a city in Ivory Coast, headquarters of many chocolate companies are present which procure almost the entire production of Ivory Coast. The CEO and officials working here strongly deny the presence of any child labour on the cocoa farms, but these words were in a direct contradiction with the ground videos, recorded just a few hours later. The investigators came across 4 little boys aged between 10-12 years, on a nearby Cocoa farm. They were originally from Burkina Faso and had never seen the face of a school. Later, they came across numerous child laborers. They also came to know about a local plantation owner, who purchased a child laborer (or better to refer them as child slaves) for 230 Euros. Further, most children don't get paid and there is a kind of a feudal attachment with the land (a scenario which was seen in Early medieval South India and later in Europe during the "Dark ages"). Sometimes these child slaves flee the plantations and if caught they are beaten up and tortured. A study by a local university suggested that child laborers employed in these plantations were 51% higher than in 2005. Apart from this, there are many reasons for employing child laborers. Low farm gate prices for cocoa beans, low farm yields per hectare due to ageing trees, infertile soil, and outdated production methods; lack of diversified incomes from sources other than cocoa are also some reasons. Furthermore, lack of child protection mechanisms; lack of quality education, and loopholes in policing (thereby a free hand to the traffickers) are a few more reasons. Similarly, there is a limited attention paid towards the vulnerable groups in the context of socio-economic inclusion. Other reasons include weak enforcement of legal and regulatory frameworks, lack of decent work opportunities, poor vocational education and skills training, and weak farm based organizations.

Then coming to case studies, out of many examples of Child laborers, there is one example of Serry Kone. He used to work 10 hours a day. One day, as his friend was taking a nap after hours of work, the plantation owner came and started thrashing him brutally. He stood up for his friend and he met the same fate. That was enough for him. He somehow escaped that den of brutality and in 2012 he founded an NGO called "Well Africa". Since 2012, the NGO has rescued 300 children out of the Cocoa farms. Not only this it has facilitated their admission in schools; provided microfinance loans to the grown-up boys and in 2014 the NGO had established its first school.

**Philosophical underline**

Child labor has many facets from an ethical point of view. Autonomy, beneficence, justice, non-malfeasance, privacy, and veracity are endangered during child labor. Utilitarianists would support the idea of child labor as long as they are the sole providers for the family because without their income, their family would not survive. The ends justify the means (from their point of view). Forced child labor is unethical because it is against the autonomy of the children. The consent of the working child is mostly manipulated by the parents. To give consent, a child needs to understand the situation, the consequences, and he/she needs to voluntarily agree for the work. Children of young age, who have a less than fully competent capacity, cannot independently assent to action by getting involved in the decision-making process. Children fall easy-victim to unfair job conditions, and they do not have the power to stand up against mistreatments. The malfeasance of this act has long-term physical, psychological, behavioral, and societal consequences. Even if they are lacking the competency of making informed decisions, they are considered individuals with autonomy.

# VIII

# BERLIN CONFERENCE: THE PAPER PARTITION OF AFRICA

Year: 1885Place: Berlin

A conference was organized by Otto Von Bismark, the first chancellor of Germany. Though the discussion had taken place for 3 months, the effective outcome was:

A huge map of Africa was kept on the conference table. The clerk was asked to bring a Pencil and a huge ruler. Few people were told to hold the map tightly against the table. And with the saliva dripping from the lips of a few, horizontal and vertical lines were drawn on the African continent (that followed the latitudes and longitudes). And after doing this acute back-breaking work, the members (representatives of European nations) of the conference began to assign the rectangular figures on the African map to the European nations represented in the conference. The process followed was: "Chitty Chitty Bang Bang which rectangle you want". "I want this.. ", came the reply. "Sure! You will get this but you naughtyy boyy!! You have to make a pinky swear that you will not ask for any part of the adjoining rectangle, because the other person may get angryy...." "Ooooon...Ok! I swear!" came the reply.

And that is how the world's fastest colonization of a continent took place. The fate of the continent was decided in a European city through a paper partition. The tribes were divided across the irrational borders of these rectangles and hence not only did the drain of African wealth (by the European nations) began but the issue of ethnic majority and minority brought a phase of incessant warfare which continues till date. Numerous issues emerged out of this mess like Rinderpest, coercive proselytization by missionaries, etc. And out of these issues, one was child Labour.

Child labour had existed in African tribes earlier but a renewed drive towards commercialization of agriculture; mining of minerals had worsened the situation and children became mere tools in these ultra-capitalistic endeavors. Now 73 million children in Africa are sent out to work, who do back-breaking labour and 85% of them work on agricultural fields. They have not only lost their youth, but also the childhood recreation; the opportunity to educate their selves for a good future; and the opportunity to think and imagine. Their self-esteem is crushed every day by their employer and many of them become quiet and withdrawn. They grow up resenting the society and they have anger beneath their hearts. Africa has one of the highest child labour rates and they work on banana fields, coffee and cocoa plantations, mines, palm oil plantations, tobacco plantations, leather industry, and where not.

**Kenya**

During the pandemic, child labour rates increased drastically in Kenya. The Nairobi quarry is full of numerous such examples. A 12-year-old girl says that she works to ensure food on the table of her house. Families are caught between a rock and a hard place. James Elder, the UNICEF spokesperson had said that the longer kids stay out of school, the more likely that they won't return.

**Sudan**

The case of Sudan and South Sudan is no different. Children are working as shoe polishers, traders, and carpenters for a meager amount of 1-1.5 dollars per day. During the civil war, apart from cattle, 20000 children were abducted, dislocated, and abused. They were forced to fight in the war and they were taught inhumane methods to torture the captives. In such pursuits, many of them were drugged and they became addicts at a young age. While the war had ended with the formation of South Sudan, the traumatic experience doesn't ends. Child soldiers were demobilized after the war; many had come back while the remaining were sold in markets. One such case is of a boy, who was abducted and sold for 50 cows. He then became a cattle herder for the purchaser family and 10 years later he was allowed to go to a distant market called Gumbo cattle market from where he escaped and returned to his shop after 10 years. His mother saw him and replied, "Yes! How may I help you.......?"

AK-47s are used to steal kids because child abduction is a good way to make money. They are sold as pseudo slaves or child laborers. There is an example of a girl who was abducted on her way to school. She was trained to do arson and torture during the war. War has ended and now she is 16. She is a mother and is getting trained in a vocational training center. Even after the war, many people are not making concrete houses as they think war is a persistent risk.

**Ethiopia**

There are more than 100 shops in Adis Ababa which sell traditional Ethiopian clothing: scarves; shorts etc, which are made by children. In the outskirts of the city, there is a small house, wherein a dark room 7 weaving looms are placed and children can be seen working. The supervisor is called Father by the children and that's how it rolls. The air of the room is suspended with "cotton fibers" and it is difficult to breathe

A local NGO called "I CARE" is working hard to rescue child labour. It gets foreign donations but it doesn't allow the interference of donors in its own work, as an attached condition. As per a survey by a local NGO called WABE, child labour has increased drastically during the pandemic times.

**Somalia**

5000 young boys live on the streets of Mogadishu and nearby gunshots are quite usual affairs for them. They wander in the streets, scrub the windshields of cars and some of them even beg. Since 1991, Somalians have lived without any government and moreover the economy is in shambles. Terrorist organizations like Al-Shabab are quite active in the region and many warlords have grown up in these fertile grounds of anarchy. Frequent famines have turned the conditions even worse.

Child labour is rampant and UN-facilitated pseudo-governance is just not sufficient to regulate and prevent child labour. Moreover, 40% of the kids are malnourished. The child laborers work in the ceramics sector, firework industries, and also in mines for a menial income of nearly 2 dollars per day. The anarchy since 1991 has reduced the income of families by nearly 60% and hence the issues like child labour have become more rampant. National development Plan by the pseudo para-statal institutions have failed to bring any significant relief and in such a scenario, 40% of the children below 15 are working in one or the other form.

**Togo**

Though the nation had committed to end Child Labour by 2021 still the issue prevails. If the stone crushing industry is considered, numerous kids are forced to crush stones into gravel. Many of them wield hammers from dusk till dawn. They talk about a drug that once injected child laborers then work like an animal across day and night. These child laborers or their parents have never heard about human rights and some of them probably will never will. The contractor at one place has an agreement with parents that their children will work from 7 A.M. - 12 P.M. and then 2 P.M. - 4 P.M. Once the gravel is sold, the parents are paid. Then reports mention that some Togolese children are also trafficked to Nigeria for unbearably hard labour. One such child mentions that they used to stay at the workplace only, where the roof was leaky and they had to sleep while standing up just like a horse. Despite all this, child laborers can be seen singing "Welcome to our beautiful village."

**Tanzania**

In Tanzania, 28% of children work. Just like Togo let's take an example of stone mining in the Utete village of Tanzania. Children were forced to drop out of schools because of dismal conditions of family and lack of social security measures and frequent droughts often worsen the situation. A child labourer says that he and his family eat morning to morning i.e. once a day. They sell 4 buckets of gravel for 2000 bucks but the labour is backbreaking. Similarly, they work in gold mines and the risks are similar as seen in cases of Peru and Burkina Faso.

In summation, child labour rates are quite high in Africa, as compared to other parts of the world and much of the issue is linked to the underdeveloped nature of economies; lack of social protection measures, etc.

**Philosophical underline**

Naidu (2012) made an effort of focusing attention on several societal and ethnic factors influencing the presence of child labor

Child labor essentially relies on normative approaches regarding children within civilization, the socially regulated parts and purposes of children, the standards through which the doings of children are considered along with the trait of socializing procedure. In developed nations, overall condemnation is there, regarding partaking of school-aged children within the official labor group. The partaking of children in household chores is accepted, according to parentages at any rate. In several nations, partaking in numerous kinds of financial actions from an early age is deemed to be a vital portion of socializing. The predominant styles of local administrations and structure of affinity influence child labor as well. What children need to do is impacted through how the structure of relationship reflects the responsibilities and rights of children. In numerous areas, the allocation of features of parent roles, along with the established exercise of nurturing of children by relations other than parents, include extensive transmissions of the responsibility for training and maintaining children along with the privilege of enjoying the facilities of the kids.

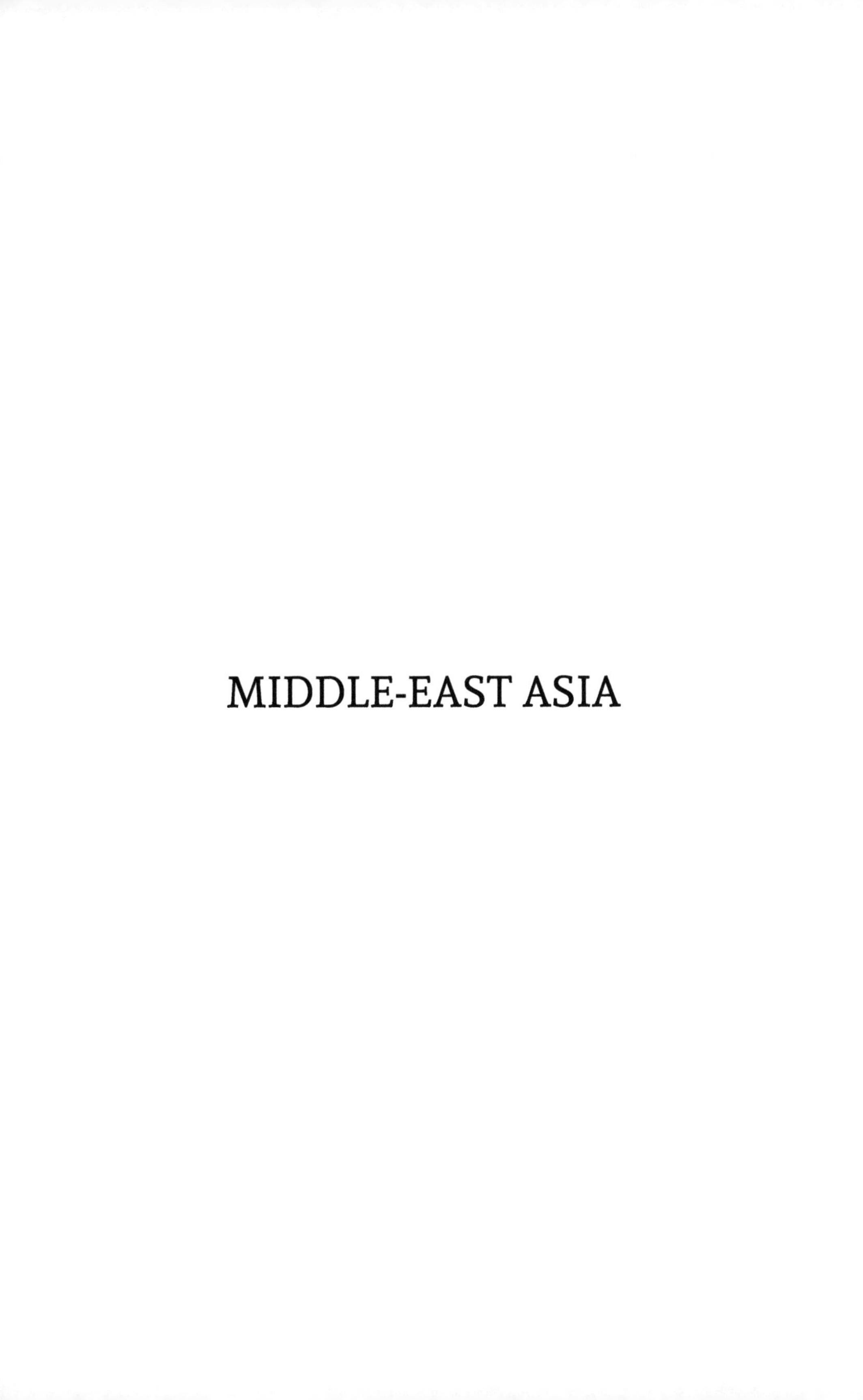

# MIDDLE-EAST ASIA

# IX

# THE CHILDREN OF GAZA STRIP

What happens when a society/nation fights for its survival?

The answer is that it fights furiously! Just recall the 30 years of the Vietnam War or the Battle of Saraighat between the Ahoms and the Mughals, and you will understand. Similar was the case with Israel. After the persecution by Nazis, Israel was the only homeland of Jews and when their existence was threatened by the surrounding Arab nations, it all boiled down to a matter of survival. Therefore be it the 1948 Israel Palestine war or the 7 days-Israel and "allied Arab" war in 1967, or the 1973 Yom Kippur war, Israel proved itself strong enough for the combined Arab power. But the result of these three wars was that the territory of Palestine got squeezed until two small patches of land were left: West Bank and Gaza strip.

Though tensions still continue to persist but Gaza has a lot more to worry about. Gaza has one of the highest population densities as compared to any patch of land on this planet. Territorial enclosure and economic blockade by Israel; limited avenues of livelihood; exploding population on a small piece of land (half the population is under 18), all these have given rise to numerous problems. Out of that, Child labour is one of the prominent issues.

7% of children aged between 10 and 17 are working in Gaza though the law bans employment below 15 years of age. The blockade imposed by Israel since 2007 has already slashed the GDP of Gaza by half. As per the Palestinian bureau of statistics, the unemployment rate in Gaza is the highest in the world (at 49%), and nearly 47% of people are food insecure.

Muhammad is 12 years old and sells goods on the streets of Gaza. He makes nearly 1.3 dollars every day. Then there is another boy who is 10 years old and who works as a mechanic. He has 7 brothers and sisters. "Parents had chosen this job for me", he says. Similarly, Hassan is 13 years old and works in a garage from 8 A.M - 8 P.M. Likewise, Mustaffa is 17 years old and he scavenges the scrap yard for metal and plastics, a job he has been doing since he was 10. The metal and plastic collected from scrap are sold to a firm.

Just nearby lives a boy named Jaber Majed. There was a time he used to go to school and used to play football but now the situation has changed. His father is a taxi driver and earns 4 dollars per week. He has 7 siblings. He reaches his garage early in the morning, sweeps it before other workers arrive. Then the work of car repair begins. He takes half an hour rest during lunch and gets back to work. "My head and my back hurt", he says. He goes back home and spends half an hour with his friend Ahmad, haves his dinner, and goes to sleep. "That is life all bout now", he says.

Beneath every story is one underlying endeavor i.e. survival. But all this comes at a cost and that is lost childhood, lost education, and lost opportunity to improve one's future. Moreover, there is a toll on well being of a child. He/ she often turn out to be aggressive, spiteful, and sometimes later on, one even starts resenting the society.

**Philosophical underline**

The occurrence of child labor is entrenched not only in socio-financial groundwork, mass destitution, illiterateness, and joblessness but also in political situations. The structure of child labor is a longstanding occurrence that hinders the growth of children because of premature service. Children toil for a diversity of motives, the majorly significant one is destitution and the provoked stress on them for escaping from this dilemma. To conclude such children are denied the humble delights of babyhood, downgraded in its place to a mere existence of labour.

# X

# THE 'SHAVEESH' OF LEBANON

Jasmine revolution or the 28-day campaign of civil resistance in Tunisia (2011) included a series of street demonstrations and this led to the ousting of the longtime President ABidine Ben Ali. This was just the beginning. A series of anti-government protests, uprisings, and armed rebellions spread across numerous other Arab nations. It was a response to economic stagnation and poor civil liberties. From Tunisia, the protests then spread to five other countries: Libya, Egypt, Yemen, Bahrain, and the infamous case of Syria!

The Syrian crisis has persisted for over a decade now. It ranks the last, amongst all nations in the IEP Peace index of the world. Millions of Syrians have left the nation, some found refuge in Europe, and some went to the adjoining nations in quest of security and peace. But amongst all the nations, Lebanon took the largest number of Syrian refugees (1.5 million). One reason was that Syria and Lebanon have had peaceful relations as they both are Shiite countries predominantly and Hezbollah of Lebanon had been a strong supporter of Assad and Syrian people. But in the Lebanese camps, the condition of Syrian refugees is nowhere near good.

It is the month of November and there is work for Syrian children on the Potato plantations of Beqaa valley (near the Syrian border). The farmer who owns the potato plantation hires the "child wage slaves" via a refugee camp supervisor called "Shaveesh". Syrian children are brought on a truck, just like animals. Men with sticks control the child laborers on the farm and gossip is not allowed. The farm owner has to be kept happy as there is no shortage of Syrian child laborers.

Syrian refugees pay traffickers for crossing the border and settling in camps and if they are not able to pay then the camp supervisor or "Shaveesh" pays for their tent, electricity, etc. His business is to house the refugees who have no residential permits, no valid documents. Whoever ends up in his custody has to obey his rules. In return, the refugees (including Syrian children) work for him and he takes part of their wages. An NGO teaches the Syrian children in the Lebanese camps.

Weam is a 13-year-old girl who works on plantations and says that she can attend the "camp school" only during rain. She attends school with junior children because she had missed a lot of school due to the Syrian crisis.

Nearby is a place called Rite where Syrians have been coming to work for decades but Syrian crisis had caused an upsurge in the Syrian laborers. Since the construction industry of Lebanon is booming, there are many concrete factories in the town. Alasly family lives in a nearby brick factory in the city. Back home, they used to run a big transport company and they had a large house but they had to migrate from Syria when a missile had struck their house. In the cement factory, 13-year old Raghad helps her brother to fill cement in mold. Ali, a 13-year-old Syrian boy works in the same factory and on being asked about his work. He says, "I hate this (and begins to cry)." In summation, circumstances have robbed them of their childhood.

Lebanese schools are already overwhelmed and Syrian kids are denied admissions via some or the other excuse. Though some Syrian teachers in Lebanon are getting funds from international groups organized by French teachers but educational efforts are just not sufficient for the Syrian children who still hope to go back home someday.

**Philosophical underline**

Jyotirmayee Kar, has shown child labor in the context of 2 kinds of restrictive features: Destitution and illiterateness. Here was is an important reason for destituteness. Also, low growth, have been recognized as the major factors influencing supply of child labor, although segment-particular labor output is observed as being a robust factor of its requirement. It has been perceived according to macro-level information that children's job input might be decreased through elevating the financial situation of the household. Bigger service in the subordinate, tertiary, and facility subdivisions, in which labor output is greater, will demonstrate to be reducing the child labour, while a greater percentage of marginal laborers along with the ones engaged in the key subdivision is observed as having a conflicting result. Developing countries like Lebanon are more tilted towards the latter.

# XI

# THE SYRIAN REFUGEES IN TURKEY

"There's a voice that now is calling,
Loudly calling, day by day;
"This the voice of right and justice,
And its tones we must obey,
We must hasten to the rescue,
Of the children young and frail,
Who are weary of their burdens,
And too soon their strength will fail
In our stores and shops, we find them,
Mid the bloom or early spring;
But the Lord is watching o'er them,
And their calls to Him we bring,
Though their parents bid them labor
And deny their needed rest;
Yet our faith believes the promise,
That their wages be redressed.
Men of rank and high position,
Men who guard our native land,
In the name of our Redeemer,
Come and lend a helping hand.
Come at once; the plea is urgent,
And the hours are waning still;
Make these children glad and happy,

And the law of love fulfill"
-Fanny Crossby

The poem titled "Hymn for the working children" aptly describes the situation of child labour and thy hymn equally applies to the Syrian refugees in Turkey. Out of the refugee spillover, a large chunk was also absorbed by the nation of Turkey, once called as "Sick man of Europe".

Nadim-al-Nako dreams of pen and a book as they are better than furnaces and the smell of diesel. He works in a refinery and his 4 siblings were killed in the civil war. He says, "We extract gases, inhale fumes and my chest feels suffocated. War destroyed our dreams and don't care about school anymore." Nearby there is a sewing workshop, where a cute 12 years old boy,. He works 12 hours a day and the rattling noise of the sewing machine seems to become the soundtrack of his childhood. Similarly, Aris and Musa are from Syria. They are 13 years and 11 years old respectively and they work in the same sewing workshop. Mother of Aris says that every morning Aris used to cry about not going to the workshop, but not it has become a habit. The employer of the workshop knows very well that employing children is a crime but he says that if he doesn't employ them, they shall be begging on the streets and he prevents financial harassment and sexual harassment. Here, at least their self-esteem is intact. Nearly 1 million Syrian refugees live in Istanbul and one-third of them are children

Similarly, Hamza and his brother work 12 hours a day and 6 days a week. He says "There is no other alternative. There is no aid, no charity. We are the breadwinners of the family. We feed our brother who cannot work." Probably he makes sense because children cannot read books with their stomachs empty. Further, there are some children, who work on the streets; collect trash and sell it to a recycling factory for nearly 6 lire (2 Euros). No doubt a Syrian organization is working in coordination with Turkish Police to rescue Syrian children from inhumane working conditions but despite all the efforts, Syrian kids continue to work.

**Philosophical underline**

Wars and disasters often have a disproportionately larger impact on vulnerable sections, and without a dint of doubt, Syrian children belong to this category. Their education is disrupted; they lose their parents; they are abducted during conflicts; they undergo trauma because they are not that mature to witness bloodshed and killings around. The issue of Child labour is closely associated with conflict situations because conflicts often disrupt the livelihood of families and subsequently the basic needs of humans like food, shelter, etc are threatened too. Therefore children often become vulnerable to the family pressures in the context of working because they are dependent on their parents, which limit the child's autonomy. This taking up of work is not determined by the child itself rather directed by other parties. And once they start working, the corresponding violation of the fundamental human rights of children conflicts with the idea of social welfare, since many types of child labourers, cause permanent damage to body and mind (given fragile bodies of children), preventing most child workers from reaching the age of 50. Additionally, beating, humiliating and psychological assault of children is opposed to any humanitarian standpoint.

# SOUTH ASIA

# XII
# THE AFGHAN SUN

Into the villages, a reminder runs dry,
Off worn mountains, by an unforgiving sky,
Each unheard whisper is a hurried breath,
Lost like water in this valley of death,
Here in the rifts, are humanities dear,
Left for abandon, and soldiers to sear,
A fate, but God has left long ago,
In its place of war, for that we don't know.
One day streams may flow and run,
Under the unforgiving sky, of the Afghan sun.
- Kerissa Morris

It is hardly a hidden truth, that C.I.A. had armed the Afghan Mujahideens during the Soviet invasion of Afghanistan (1979 -89). These very Mujahideens later formed the Taliban and the irony was that later, U.S.-dominated NATO had to spend almost two decades on the same Afghan soil, to fight its very own creation Taliban. But eventually, NATO troops had to leave Afghan soil in 2021 with the immediate result of the Taliban takeover of Afghanistan.

But amidst all these war years, the economy of Afghanistan was the hardest hit. The infrastructure was destroyed, trade was disrupted and agriculture suffered too. The result is that issues like poverty and debt are widespread. Child labour is widely prevalent and nearly 30% of kids between 5 and 16 years of age are working.

Here are some investigations, done before the US retreat.

Azizullah, a cute boy with red cheeks is 12 years old and he works as a carpet weaver in a workshop in Kabul. He says with an innocent smile, "I work from 5 in the morning to 6 in the evening." Children working here are suffering from Carpal Tunnel syndrome due to overwork, diminishing vision, and dust from yarn causes a frequent cough, and lastly the back pain is a persistent problem. Similarly, numerous other kids work as shoe shiners, mechanics, bonded laborers in brick kilns (as their parents have to pay a debt to the brick kiln owners). Helal Sajjad, a 13-year-old kid works in a metal beating workshop. He shows a deep cut on his leg and some cuts on his hands too. He wakes up every day with Masjid's call to prayer and works for 12 hours a day.

A few months ago, a boy named Haseeb (A mechanic) was working below a car, somehow the jack faltered and he was immediately killed. Nearby there lives a 13-year-old boy named Pervez. He works as a shoe shiner because his father doesn't even earn 20 Afghanis a day. Every day he goes out with his friends (all working as shoe shiners). They walk on the streets asking shop owners for shoe polish. They stick together because there is competition from other boys and there is a threat of getting beaten up. Pervez earns 70 Afghanis per day. He says, "We have to do this because a sack of wheat costs 2000 bucks and a jug of cooking oil costs 3000 bucks." Many a day he has to return empty hand. While walking through the streets, he passes across the Kebab shop; he is hungry but cannot purchase a Kebab. Then luck strikes as he finds a customer. The person says that doesn't needs to get his shoes polished; he just wants to see a smile on their faces, hence he gets it done. With the money earned, they buy a single piece of bread and they share it amongst themselves. In summation, Kabul is no place to be young for the destitute.

Zia Khan a mother of 7 cries while talking, as she is a widow and her youngest one is sick and other sons are laboring hard for her family's survival. Not far away is the house of Sahib Khan, who is an educated school teacher and he is ready to sell her daughter due to gruesome economic situations. "I am not able to take care of her", he says with pain right visible in his eyes. 40% of crops are lost this year and there is a condition of near starvation in some regions.

The national budget is mostly spent on security and hence social issues cannot be well focused upon. Further with sanctions imposed on the Taliban; with international funding cut; with foreign reserves frozen; the condition is bound to get worse.

**Philosophical underline**

It is commonly said that all children are born free and equal but it needs to be called into question because a child is conceived in a social context and born into a social context. The prevailing social conditions have their effect on the child, right from birth and maybe even earlier. Every child is a link in civilization. The link always has continuity with the past and it can also muster the powers to break with the past within certain limits. The rights of the child become relevant in relation, to the past and even the future. Due to the vulnerability of children, they are prone to exploitation, and child labor is one of the worst forms where a child is helpless to perform the responsibilities of adults in his childhood for survival. Unfortunately, there are some children, who are born only to work. Hence a vicious circle of poverty is formed and the phenomenon of child labor is reborn after every generation.

# XIII

# PAKISTAN: THE PROVINCE OF BALUCHISTAN

Baluchistan, a province of Pakistan forms nearly 44% of the area of Pakistan. It had always been uncomfortably sandwiched between the great Persian and Indian empires. In the $11^{th}$ century, Seljuk Turks invaded Persia and hence began the eastward migration of the nomadic tribes (today Balochs). Baluchistan gradually came under the rule of Kalat and after the attack of the British, it became an associate state of the British in 1854. Finally, in 1948, it became a part of Pakistan. It is a region that remains neglected and ignored. As a result, it is an insurgency-stricken area (with some wars fought in 1958-59, 1963, and a major one between 1973 and 1977). Amongst many other reasons, a major cause of conflict between Balochs and the Government of Pakistan is Baloch accusations of the economic exploitation of the region. As a result, there is high unemployment and inflation, and amongst many associated problems, one is the issue of child labour.

Karachi may be the highest revenue-generating city of Pakistan but there is a grim side of the city. Numerous working children can be seen on the streets, in workshops, as domestic help, as Kulfi sellers, etc. A 12-years-old boy works in a small concrete industry. He makes 300 concrete blocks and earns Rs 150 per day. His mother is ill and one tablet cost Rs 50. His mother says, "We don't get any ration, and inflation has broken our backs."

A working boy complains that his "ustaad" hits him with slippers and also hits hammers on his legs if he finds any laxity. He works more than 10 hours a day and earns Rs 50 per day. Similarly, there are some children, who find food in the nearby garbage dump, where leftover from restaurants is dropped. Shivers go deep down the spine on seeing such dismal sights because, in a food web, a similar role is played by scavengers who feed upon the leftover. Moreover, children are very vulnerable to diseases like Hepatitis A. But yes there are alternatives too! Some parents send their kids to a nearby Madrassah and educating their kid is not a priority rather the main concern is that Madrassa will provide food to their kid and at least they will not sleep empty with stomachs. When two child laborers (brothers) were interviewed to find their reasons for working, the smaller one says, "Maa-baap ke vaaste karte hain (we do it for our parents)" and begins to cry while the elder brother embraces him.

Further, distressed people often accuse that national and international funds do not reach the right place due to rampant corruption. As per the All Pakistan survey 2011, 21 million children were indulged in labour work, though law bans employment below 14 years of age and free education is guaranteed for children aged between 5 to 16 years of age.

In other provinces, there are laws like Khyber Pakhtunwah Child Labour ban Act 2017 and Punjab Child labour ban act 2015, but the ground realities are still far from desired. Coming back to the case of Baluchistan, as per the ILO report in 2013, nearly 500 children were working in coal mines of Loralai district. Similarly, SEHR reported that 10,000 child laborers were present in Quetta.

Then let's talk about CPEC. It is a joint Pak-Chinese road and rail project that gives Chinese goods quicker access to the Arabian Sea which earlier required a big turnaround through the Malacca Strait. It is a constant source of friction between India and Pakistan, as the road passes through POK which Indian claims as its territory. But apart from the political tensions, this project came into the limelight for one more reason i.e. the use of child labour. While writing this book I came across numerous interviews and case studies but to be honest, I just couldn't control my tears while seeing a 7-year-old kid pushing a heavy boulder somewhere on this CPEC project. His father had died 2 years ago and he works with his brother. The contractor pays their mother for the labour of her sons. It is their daily routine to load heavy boulders on a trawley (again driven by a kid).

It is quite ironic to find child laborers just near the Baluchistan assembly. Just nearby, an interesting incident had taken place. A local labour inspector had raided a workshop and had rescued child laborers; the employer was arrested and was brought before the court. The parents of child laborers argued in favor of the employer and asked the judge to release him. In summation and as evident from other parts of world, Child labour is driven by the dire needs of the family. The effectiveness of the "Child labour ban" law is highly doubtful especially when the governments are not able to provide social security to the vulnerable families. It may be harsh but it's simple! a hungry family struggling for survival can never obey the 'child labour ban' laws. No progressive society wants to see this menace of child labour, but conditions have to be created, social security must be provided before we seek to enforce child labour laws in heart and spirit.

**Philosophical Underline**

No matter how despicable child labor is, it provides impoverished families a vital source of income for their survival. Simultaneously, since the work occupies the entire time, children often are unable to receive basic education, a deficit that leads to high opportunity costs accounting to an 11% loss of income per missed school year, which will deprive the family of higher long-term earnings. Beyond that, as being aware of the terrible working conditions their children are exposed to, parents are most likely plagued by accusations and pity. Moreover quest for freedom and happiness are two important driving impulses for the evolution of human civilization but child laborers lack both these attributes. Further, if this menace has to be dealt with, then change has to be brought from within the society because no amount of compliance and governance, can substitute a sound moral fiber.

# INDIA: THE CASE OF UTTAR PRADESH

# XIV

# MORADABAD BRASS: FROM 'JHALAI' TO 'RAGDAI'

Moradabad district in Uttar Pradesh is known to have one of the largest brassware manufacturing units in the country. The brass industry is structurally fragmented and it can be broadly divided into three segments: exporters/traders, artisans, and middlemen/agents. Women and children constitute 10 and 5 percent of the total, labour force respectively. There is almost no contact between the traders and the artisans. The exporters/traders hold the level of control, both as suppliers of raw material and sellers of finished products. The agents called Bhartiyas take the order from the exporters. The Karigars constitute unskilled, semi-skilled, and skilled workers. The Karigars work at the household level, either as part of the family or as wage earners. And these Karigars further employ children to lower the production cost.

Children are involved in numerous activities. First is the process of 'Dhalai', where children rotate the cycle wheel that fans the furnace and they put ingots into a crucible containing molten brass. The second is the Chillai, where scrapping is done on power-operated lathes. The third is the Jhalai, where children hold the pieces together for welding via the use of gas cylinders. Fourth is the Ragdai, i.e. washing and polishing the brass articles to give them the requisite gloss. Washing is done by children in a mixture that has hydrochloric acid and polishing is carried out in buffing machines.

There are numerous health hazards for children. They stand near the furnaces bare feet which often lead to severe burn injuries. The children also inhale the fumes and gases which are let off from the furnace. Similarly, during welding, the main worker wears colored goggles but the helper who is generally a child, observes the glare with bare eyes which has a damaging effect on the eyes. Further children can be seen sitting on cylinders in these welding workshops which may blast any time with a single mistake. Most of these children belong to 6-9 year age group. Not only this, fumes arising from acid tubes often lead to nausea and vomiting. Similarly, unhygienic living and working conditions combined with malnutrition makes them vulnerable to communicable diseases. Further, contact dermatitis is a health hazard seen in children working in processes where chemicals are used, especially potassium cyanide, silver nitrate, and ammonium chloride in the electroplating process. Further, Ankylosis, Spondylitis, and permanent spinal deformities have been attributed to abnormal posture, which the working children have to adapt while working.

# XV
# THE ALIGARH LOCK

Aligarh is well known for its traditional product: the ubiquitous lock. This lock manufacturing industry is organized in such a way that some processes are carried out in factory premises and the remaining parts get manufactured through contractors or middlemen, whereas final assembly takes place in the factory. While the lock industries owned by the brand owner manufacturers are equipped with the modern technology of production, the contractors or middlemen employ artisans. Though these artisans are employed regularly by the contractors, they are paid by piece rate. The artisans in turn employ children as helpers. Since most of the artisans are illiterates, they are unaware of the trends in the market and usually end up incurring losses. Moreover, the artisans are not in a strong bargaining position with regard to the price of the output and they have to sell the locks to the middlemen at less remunerative prices. Therefore the only way to survive in the competitive business of lock production is to rely heavily on cheap labour.

A study was conducted, which reveals that children constitute 45% of the total workforce in the lock industry. Of the working children, 70% were employed as individual workers, and the remaining 30% work as a part of the family.

Children are involved in numerous activities throughout the process. An extremely hazardous activity where more than 70% of the workers are children below the age of 14 years is the process of electroplating. Children are engaged in tying polished metal pieces on copper wires, which are then strung on rods and submerged in alkaline baths. Children are found using various solutions with bare hands containing chemicals like potassium cyanide, trisodium phosphate, etc. Electric current passes through chemical tanks and children often get electric shocks. Similarly, rusted pieces of metal are polished on buff machines. The bobs on these machines are covered with emery powder. The face of the worker is within 10 inches of rotating machines that run on power.

Breathing problem occurs among children involved in Buff polishing, drum polishing, and spray painting the locks. Further inhaling the mixture of emery powder and metal dust causes tuberculosis. Moreover, during spray painting, the paint thinner enters their body gradually and accumulates. It leads to nausea, breathing problems, and lung cancer. Children engaged in the electroplating process suffer from skin and heart diseases. Their fingertips get grazed while working in hand press and power press. Children are not alert sometimes due to fatigue and long working hours and accidents happen more often.

# XVI

# LUCKNOW ZARI: THE MUGHAL HERITAGE

Zari making is a heritage craft with its roots in Mughal times. The craft has a huge demand both in the domestic and export markets. The industry is organized on a three-tier basis, where the power lies mainly in the hands of big businessmen and exporters. At the top of the system are manufacturers and traders. They finance the production by supplying the necessary materials. Each manufacturer or trader is associated with a Karkhanedar (at times he is also a commission agent) who gets the work done through Karigar(artisan). Being a traditional craft-based occupation with a closed labour market, the skill passes from one generation to another.

Since the skill required in Zari making and all the related processes are not changing, children of the Karigars seem to develop an understanding of the craft at an early age, as they witness it being done at their homes or otherwise. One year of training is enough for a child to become a Karigar(artisan), thus adding to the family income as a regular wage earner. Employers benefit by employing children since their wage rate is more flexible than the adults. Moreover, children basically work as apprentices and therefore a full-fledged wage is not paid.

There are numerous reasons for the high employment rate of children. Static technology, with a low level of productivity coupled with low-income levels, generates a situation in which the demand for child labor is high. Secondly, the trade, in a majority of the cases is confined to home-based units. Children learn a craft in their home or in the nearby Karkhanas (workshops) at a very early age. Then employers benefit as the wage rate is more flexible and lower than the adults. Apart from this: large family size, the high dropout rate from primary schools, etc are, some of the other reasons.

There are several health-related consequences. First, the issue which is normally faced by the children is related to their eyesight because of excessive strain involved in carrying out the craft. The rooms often lack sufficient light which adds up to their strain. Children also suffer from backache caused by constantly sitting in a particular posture in order to carry out the embroidery. They sit for hours together on the floor with frames raised up to the chest level for doing embroidery work. As the children are involved in the work from an early age, they neither have time for any physical activity necessary at their age nor are they able to take up any alternate employment, once they grow up. The majority of them become incapable of carrying out any work when they are around the age of forty.

# XVII

# FEROZABAD: THE GENETIC DAMAGE

Ferozabad (Uttar Pradesh, India) is quite famous for its glassware and glass bangle industry. However, while its products are renowned, the area is famous for the involvement of children in the production process of different glassware items. Ferozabad produces many products like bangles, chandeliers, crockery bulbs, wine glasses, etc.

The factory floor employs about 8,000 to 50,000 children as young as 8 years old. The factory floor is typically an inferno due to intense heat. Moreover, there is poor ventilation, broken glass, dangling electric wires, and no protective equipment.

There are numerous reasons for the employment of child labour. The glass and bangle industry is technologically backward and the pressure on workers is tremendous. Moreover, technology is obsolete and primitive glass melting technique is used. The average size of a household is 5.8 and a large family size is closely, if not exclusively, related to the issue of child labour. Further literacy levels are low (as per the 2011 census).

Children are involved in activities like Jhalai i.e. bringing the cut ends of the glass spiral in level with each other. The workers along with their family members or with some hired workers join the edges of the bangles at the home level. They sit facing each other in a row of burners. After the bangles are joined they are sent to Pakai Bhattis (furnaces) to harden them. Subsequent processes include Katai i.e. cutting or creating grooves on the bangles, colouring, and sorting.

Numerous health hazards are associated with these processes. Children may be seen working at 40-50 degrees Celsius temperature which makes them vulnerable to breathing problems like bronchitis. Watery eyes have also been observed as one of the health problems usually because of fumes and temperature differences. Tuberculosis levels are also high amongst children. Moreover, since children work with bare hands, skin burns are very common. Not only this, studies conducted by Maulana Azad college in new Delhi, showed genetic damage in the body cells of the laborers working close to furnace heat for three years, that seems true also, as many children suffer from mental retardation.

# XVIII
# RAMPURI 'CHAAKU'

Rampur district is known for its knives, identified as 'Rampuri'. The majority of the households are engaged in knife making. Large no. of children are engaged in the manufacture of a knife. At the top of the industry are knife sellers, who place an order, by mentioning type and size to the manufacturer, quite often by advancing money. The manufacturer in turn procures raw material, passes the raw material through machining processes (but without finishing the product). The knives then go back to the seller, who then sends them for nickel and polish.

Child labour continues to exist due to high demand for children as a cheap substitute for adult labour. All the households engaged in child labour belong to Rampur. Not to speak of migrants, there is not even intrusion of locals from other professions into knife making. The knife making thus remains a closely confined craftsmanship within families and groups of families inter-connected by process dependence or limited market.

There are no middle or large-scale manufacturing units; all are tiny ones at the household level, whether registered or unregistered. The scope for the engagement of child labour is higher in such units. Income from the knife industry is not sufficient to look forward to, be it the manufacturers or sellers. Hence child labour as a cheap source of labour is an option to bring down the production cost. Moreover, the knife industry has never been declared as an industry therefore it neither features in district industries list nor in the list of Labour department. Hence it is difficult to enforce any child labour legislation. And the conventional supply-side reasons are same like big families; high child population in the region as there is predominance in 6-11 years age group; less number of schools in the region etc.

There are numerous processes involved in knife making like Farma design or design of knife (engraved on wood). The second is Dhalai, where raw material is melted in the furnace and then molded. Then comes the process of Gharai i.e. blade making work which is done by a specialist only. Fourth is Jarai, wherein the blade and engraved handle are joined together. Lastly, there is a process of Uttrai or sharpening the edges and then polishing, a work performed only by specialists.

In all these processes children are engaged as helpers. While making the blade children are used to fan the furnace. They gradually inhale the fume arising from the furnace and they usually get infected with various respiratory diseases like Asthama, Bronchitis, etc. Constant exposure to harmful chemicals makes them vulnerable to tuberculosis too. Similarly while polishing the handle with silvery-white metallic elements, sometimes children also consume it orally and it may cause lung cancer. Lastly working for long hours, poverty and malnourishment further degenerate their growth and development.

# XIX

# THE SLAUGHTER HOUSES

There are two main types of slaughterhouses operating, organized and unorganized. Illegal slaughtering is done at many places in Uttar Pradesh. Most of the child labour belongs to migrant households, who migrated due to poverty and unemployment. Many children working in slaughterhouses are runaway children. When they do not find any other work in a new place and situation, they join the labour force in the slaughterhouse either directly or through a relative already working there. Children work for around 9-10 hours a day and working at night is a regular feature with no provision of overtime wages or facilities for medication, ventilation, illumination, toilet, etc

There are numerous factors behind this scenario. This is an export-oriented industry. The abattoirs in India export meat to the Middle East, including Saudi Arabia, UAE, Qatar, Oman, etc. Alongside, the skin, hides, and other by-products also make a significant contribution to the economy. Further, by-products from slaughterhouses are used in the preparation of animal feeds. And the reasons in the context of the supply-side are the same as seen in previous cases.

There are numerous processes where children are employed/engaged like loading and unloading of cattle; keeping watch over poultry and animals to be slaughtered; slaughtering the animals and removing the hide; cleaning intestines; making pieces; selling meat and are also engaged as Hakais (driving the cattle from the market to the slaughtered platforms).

There are numerous problems associated with child laborers. While slaughtering the animals or making pieces these children get injured. Some children also get injured while loading or unloading the cattle. Similarly, removing the hide or cleaning the intestines of the slaughtered animals may cause respiratory problems. Moreover, slaughterhouses or their surroundings usually stink badly and this stinking smell usually causes nausea or headache. Not only this, being exposed to the process of killing continuously, they might get frightened initially but gradually they get used to it and at a later stage, these children start watching the process of slaughtering the animals as a fun activity. Lastly, a feeling of insecurity, inferiority, and low self-esteem gets deeply ingrained in their mindset.

# XX

# MIRZAPUR: THE 'KALEEN' INDUSTRY

Districts of Uttar Pradesh like Mirzapur, Sant Ravi Das Nagar, Varanasi, Allahabad, Kaushambhi, Jaunpur, and Sonbhadra are well known for the carpet-weaving industry. The socio-economic profile of these districts reflects a high density of population, low literacy rate, high infant mortality rate, and marginal land holdings with high poverty rates. Yet it accounts for 85% of all the carpets exported from India. But this industry extensively uses child labour as a cheap source of labour, to maximize their profits.

At present, there are different kinds of child laborers, those who work as a part of the family and those working on other people's loom, but from the same village or neighboring villages. Migrant child labour is also procured from distant villages of Uttar Pradesh or the neighboring state of Bihar or the foothills of Nepal. More than 90% of families working in this sector were once migrants.

Contractors make periodic trips to distant villages for procuring child laborers and they usually give an advance to the concerned families, to be later adjusted against the child's wages. Children may labour hard for years but they earn very little. Each individual knot has to be made by hand and children do eighty percent of the knotting work. Children also provide a cheap substitute for adult labour. They usually overwork and are underpaid. By and large, in most cases, a large number of working children work for longer hours per day in order to attain a given income level.

There are numerous activities where children are involved like Kabli i.e. making balls from wools; knotting and cutting; Berai or packing the knots in the right position and some other processes like bleaching, drying, and shearing.

But these activities are associated with numerous health issues for children. Weaving or knotting involves woolen threads as per the given design. Utmost concentration is required and eyes need to be fixed with both the hands half raised. There is no movement of the body. Sitting like this for several hours weakens the eyesight, makes the digestive system weak, and also turns the fingers infirm. Moreover, children inhale woolen particles which lead to respiratory diseases and lung infections. Moreover, the use of dyes and chemicals causes skin problems.

# XXI

# RAG PICKING: THE CHILD SCAVENGERS

Urbanization levels are increasing in India and these cities produce tonnes of waste every day. Therefore the number of dumping grounds is also increasing rapidly. Moreover, there is a demand to clean them and here the role of rag pickers becomes prominent. Many production enterprises in the recycling business depend upon wastes collected by the rag-picking children. Today rag picking and scavenging is a means of survival for thousands of children.

A substantial proportion of the rag-picking households are migrants, and the reason reported is mainly poverty and unemployment. Being migrants, they are subjected to all forms of exploitation of big cities. For survival, they take up occupation where there is an easy entry and rag picking is one of them.

Family size becomes significant when the earnings of the parents are below subsistence level and children are expected to supplement the family income. The literacy level is found to be very low among the rag-picking households. It seems as if illiteracy has been inherited by these children involved in rag picking. The reason behind leaving school and joining work is to supplement the family income.

Rag picking comes in the category of self-employment. The role of middlemen, called junk dealers becomes more important here. These middlemen exploit a large number of the rag pickers. Rag picking pays more than any other form of child labour in India. Though the children do not have any fixed timing in this work. Most of them start by 5 to 6 A.M. and continue till they have collected sufficient scrap to be sold to the junk dealer.

Therefore they are involved in the collection of mirrors, glasses, and other wastes including hospital wastes like blood-stained bandages, syringes, saline bottles, surgical and lab wastes which often endanger their health. They are more vulnerable to diseases like mumps, Tuberculosis, stomach infections, Tetanus, etc. The broken glasses lying in the garbage dump may injure their bare-foot and the injury may develop into deeper wounds. Many of the garbage children die of curable diseases that go uncured. They are highly vulnerable to all kinds of abuses like physical abuse, sexual abuse, etc.

# XXII
# BIDI INDUSTRY

Districts like Allahabad, Mau, Azamgarh, and Gazipur (Uttar Pradesh, India) are quite famous for Bidi manufacturing. Most of the Bidi manufacturing takes place at home. Bidi workers are provided raw materials and wages are paid on piece rate. A distinct feature of this industry is that many children work as bonded laborers. They work for contractors hired by the big Bidi-making companies. Sometimes they work full night and are maltreated too, unless the debt is paid. Parents cannot raise their voices against the exploitation and have to often keep their mouths shut.

There are numerous reasons for the employment of children. Employers are of the opinion that children have amazing grasping power and they learn quickly. Moreover, an adult can make 2500 Bidis per day and a child can make 4000 Bidis per day. Also, employing children is the cheapest form of labour and this brings down the production cost. Further, parents have a positive attitude towards agents or contractors who employ children because they often know them personally and they have faith that their child shall be properly taken care of. But the reality is that child undergoes all forms of exploitation. He or she is abused verbally and physically. If they are caught taking a small nap or gossiping they are scolded or sometimes beaten by the employer. The majority of the bonded laborers are from backward castes, and the level of illiteracy is high. Further contractors prefer employing girls below 12 years because they are more disciplined and easily can be exploited for work.

Children begin with their jobs by first assisting the already working Bidi rollers by tying cotton thread on the rolled Bidi. Often this is an unpaid job. There prevails a system of pledging the services of children in Bidi industry due to the persistence of extreme poverty among workers. Moreover, there is a practice of adult workers giving advances to children which restricts them from seeking employment elsewhere and therefore it binds the children to a particular worker. The middleman undertakes distribution of raw material and they collect the finished Bidis on behalf of an employer. Unfair practices are resorted to in this process by not accounting for Bidis rolled by workers and hence sometimes they manipulate the figures. Wages are also deducted for producing cheap quality Bidis which are taken out indiscriminately during the process of sorting. In summation, Bidi industry is characterized by low wages, uncertainty, and insecurity of employment.

Children are involved in many activities like tying thread on the rolled Bidi; closing the upper ends of rolled Bidi; leaf-cutting and Bidi rolling. There are numerous health hazards associated with the above activities. Usually, small rented dwelling houses are used for Bidi making and children usually have defective sitting posture and hence stunted physical growth. A defective sitting posture usually causes back pain and arthritis. And quite strangely, neonatal and infant deaths are reported amongst women who have been involved in Bidi making from their childhood. Children inhale as well as absorb the pulverized tobacco through palm muscles which further causes numerous health problems.

# XXIII

# KHURJA: 600 YEAR OLD POTTERY INDUSTRY

The pottery industry of Khurja is 600 years old. Children are enrolled in this industry by their guardians in the name of teaching traditional skills. However, when learning traditional skills interferes with well being of the child, it amounts to child labour and this is what is happening in Khurja. There are numerous reasons for the menace of child labor. First, illiteracy levels are quite high. Second, a population explosion has been seen in Khurja in the last few decades. Third, numerous women have reported that their husbands drink regularly and sink a major portion of earnings in it. Addiction to liquor causes further poverty and forces women and children to enter in labour market. Fourth, the majority of the child labour households are landless or peasants have marginal lands which is another determinant in child labour. Fifth, there is an issue of irregular wage payment to adults. The minimum wage has not surfaced as an issue but wages are not paid on time. Therefore the child is forced to work, to supplement the family income.

The work performed by children is locally known as "Utthai Rakhai" and consists of carrying empty mold to workers on the machine and carrying the filled mold out in the sun to dry. The child labour doing this work is called Phantiwala. A Phantiwala effectively runs about 5 kilometers a day with a ten-kilogram load. As a result, children as young as 8 or 9 years weigh up to twenty kilograms. They do numerous activities like carrying lumps of clay to Kataiwalas (who makes pot on the jigger machine); carrying half-dry pots to workers engaged in finishing work; removing handles from the molds; cutting handles to the required size and some are engaged in scrapping the rough edges.

There are numerous health problems involved with these activities. Most of the children suffer from silicosis. It is pulmonary fibrosis caused by the inhalation of dust containing free silica. Silicosis has no cure and it has been identified as an occupational disease. Moreover, children assisting the firemen in kilns often complain about cough and cold. Furthermore, a child, on average runs five kilometers a day with a 10 kg load. Their bodies bend and frames tremble with the effort. Similarly, children while removing pebbles, have their knees deep in clay which also causes skin infections.

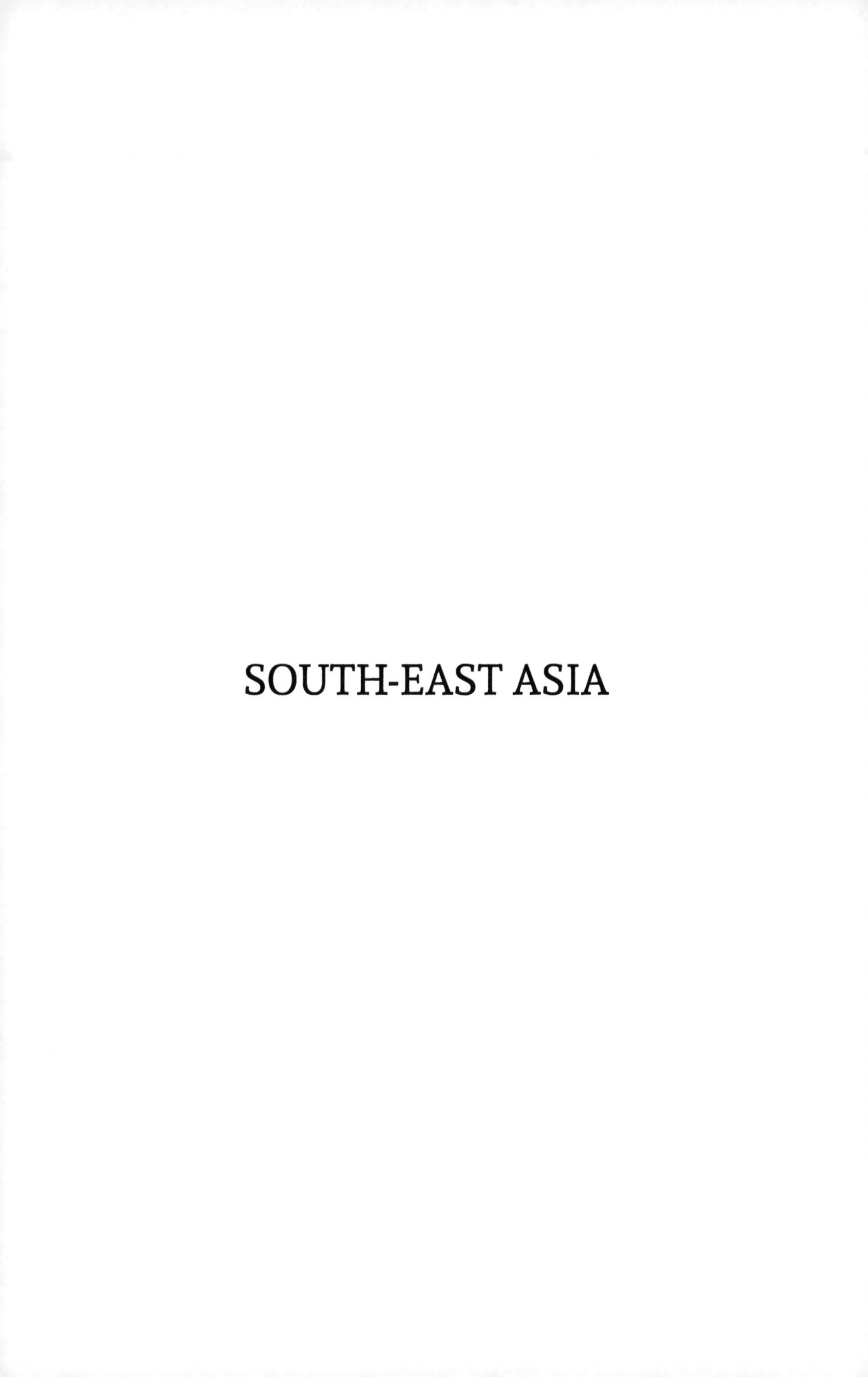

# SOUTH-EAST ASIA

# XXIV

# BANGLADESH: THE STREETS OF DHAKA

On 16 December 1971, the map of South Asia was changed and a new country was born. The result of the 1970 elections was denounced by the politicians from West Pakistan and a crackdown was launched by the West Pakistani Army upon the Bangladeshis. As a result, refugee influx increased into India, and Airfields of India were bombed by the Pakistan Air Force. India responded back and after 13 days of the war, 93000 soldiers of West Pakistan surrendered and that's how Bangladesh was born.

Now Bangladesh is one of the fastest-growing south Asian economies. The country is well known for its textiles, financial inclusion models, etc. But like many South Asian economies, it is still struggling with issues like Child Labour. As per UNICEF, children comprise 13% of the workforce and half of the Bangladeshis earn less than 2 dollars a day.

Babu is a 12-year old boy in Dhaka, he works as a porter; carries the luggage of people to make a living. He sleeps on the streets and aggrieves that while he sleeps, sometimes other street boys steal his hard-earned money. Nearby there is a beauty parlor, where a 14-year-old girl named Airen Akhtar works for a living. Just a few miles away is a cigarette manufacturing factory, where a young girl Mussamat Khatun makes cigarette wraps and also goes to school. Just to the southwest, there is a boy called Shibo who works as a mechanic. He earns nearly 18 dollars per month but doesn't complain about the job. He says, "I am gaining skills and it's my dream to set up the biggest workshop in the city." He also goes to a vocational training center to upgrade his skills. His employer knows very well that employing kids aged below 14, can fetch him a 60 dollar fine but he is not worried as the law is widely disobeyed. A few blocks away, there is a girl named Ayesha who sells newspapers and if she doesn't, then her mother beats her. Her mother used to work as a child and now she wants her to work too. A few kilometers north, there is a glass factory where a boy named Jehangir works. He works in 4 shifts throughout the day and the working conditions are horrible. He spends his day near a giant boiling furnace, hot pipes, hot glasses and he has suffered burns multiple times. And just nearby is a stone-crushing workshop where 14-year-old girl Mina works. She crushes the stone and shows numerous scars on her hands and wrists.

**Philosophical underline**

The misery of children cannot go unnoticed; the exploitation of children becomes a silent scourge that leaves its scars not only on the victims but on the several generations to come. Those children are even more vulnerable whose parents are socio-economically vulnerable and dependent on others for their survival and sustenance. Child labour has many aspects. It refers to work that is mentally, physically, socially, and morally dangerous and is harmful to children and interferes with schooling by obliging them to leave the school prematurely or requires them to attempt to combine school attendance with excessively long and heavy work. Child labour includes children permanently leading adult lives, working long hours for low wages under conditions damaging to their health and their physical and mental development, sometimes separated from their families, frequently deprived of meaningful educational and training opportunities that could open up for them a better future.

# XXV

# MYANMAR AND CAMBODIAN STORIES

"I know what the caged bird feels, alas!
When the sun is bright on the upland slopes;
When the wind stirs soft through the springing grass,
And the river flows like a stream of glass;
When the first bird sings and the first bud opes,
And the faint perfume from its chalice steals—
I know what the caged bird feels!
I know why the caged bird beats his wing
Till its blood is red on the cruel bars;
For he must fly back to his perch and cling
When he fain would be on the bough a-swing;
And a pain still throbs in the old, old scars
And they pulse again with a keener sting—
I know why he beats his wing!
I know why the caged bird sings, ah me,
When his wing is bruised and his bosom sore,—
When he beats his bars and he would be free;
It is not a carol of joy or glee,
But a prayer that he sends from his heart's deep core,
But a plea, that upward to Heaven he flings—
I know why the caged bird sings!"

*-P.L. DUNBAR*

Myanmar is a nation where nearly 130 ethnicities reside. Nearly 97% of the population is Buddhist. It was colonized by the British in the year 1886 and became independent in 1948. After its short democratic tenure beginning in 2015, the military junta again took over in November 2020.

Like many other South Asian countries, Child labour is rampant and Myanmar ranks amongst the worst performing nations. Of the children working; 60% of the children drop out from school before the age of 11. In Yangon, child laborers can be seen working on tea stalls for menial incomes. Just nearby there is a construction site where a 9-year-old boy works 7 days a week (5 AM- 7 PM) in near slave-like conditions. After high school, there is a famous entrance exam for a diploma, which as per the survey, 85% of students fail to clear. A 16-year-old teenager says, "Since I have failed to qualify for the exam, I will have to take up a hard labour job which I could have opted for 5 years before."

Apart from the conventional areas of child labour, there are different features too in Myanmar. It is also an insurgency-stricken nation. Be it the Kachin state or Rakhine state, numerous insurgent groups are active in the region and there are pieces of evidence about the recruitment of child soldiers. Moreover, Myanmar is a part of the "Golden Triangle" nations (Myanmar-Laos-Thailand), known for drug smuggling. Quite often children are used in this narcotic supply chain. Then there is an issue of child sex trafficking from Myanmar to Thailand. Burmese Children are sold in Thailand to meet the demands of tourists who come there for sex vacations. There are many channels and routes of smuggling as Myanmar has a long border with Thailand. Apart from this, there are allegations that the military junta deliberately doesn't promote higher education. The veracity of such allegations might be contestable but one thing that cannot be refuted is that the education system of Myanmar is not good enough and needs up-gradation.

**Cambodia**

Just to the east of Myanmar lies the country of Cambodia. If we look at the brick factories of Cambodia, we find numerous examples of child labourers. Rattana is 12-year-old and she works in a brick factory in Phnom Penh where she makes bricks and loads them into the trucks. She started working when she was 8. There are near slave-like conditions in brick factories. ILO spokesperson Simran Singh says, "The nature of work in brick factories would appear to be fit under ILO definitions, to be called the worst form of Child Labour."While saying this, he is not exaggerating his statement, because if we consider this brick factory in Phnom Penh then there is almost debt bondage of families. There are examples where families owe nearly 1000 dollars to the Brick owner and they stay at the construction site only where sanitation facilities are minimal. Family members (including children as young as 8) work in his brick kiln and they pay 25 dollars every month to the kiln owner as a repayment of debt installment.

Not far away is the famous lake of Tonle Sap which is South East Asia's largest lake and world's most productive inland fishery, but its productivity is endangered by increasing environmental degradation and human pressure. Fisheries are an important source of livelihood and nutrition. Chhum Kimseak helps her family with safe fishing that doesn't hamper her education and health. She peels the fish for her mother and she processes it further for sale. She presents an example of "family labour", which is still acceptable as far as one's education is not affected.

**Philosophical underline**

Work may become an unbearable burden and a risk to children while their education is neglected. In such a situation, work predominates and places children under severe stress. It endangers their healthy development and prospects of growth and overall well-being. It is in this context that child labour is considered exploitative and abusive. In other words, the work that impinges on a child's right to education, play, leisure, besides his mental, physical, spiritual, and psychological development is child labour.

# XXVI

# PHILIPPINES: BITTEN BY THE LURE OF CITY

"Wretched poverty stares.
Sternly at his face,
Compelling him to toil,
With exertion and foil,
Losing childhood joy,
Discarding shame and coy,
Deprived of learning,
In course of earning"
-Geetima Baruah Sarma

Jay and Eric are 16 and 14 years old. They have dropped out of school and they work in Paracale Gold mine without any protective gear. Dynamite is often used in the mine. Eric takes the heavy load of rock to the surface and the mining rope is manually operated during power outages. Sometimes the rain floods the mine but the work never stops. Further the chemicals are drained not only into the nearby river but also into the groundwater. Eric says, "I do the work of two people because I have 8 mouths to feed in my family." He dreams of finding a stable job to support his family.

Marie Lu was recruited from a peasant village by a rich businessman in Manila. She was beaten, harassed, and molested. A local social worked then rescued her and the matter was brought before the court and the culprit was brought to justice. Now, she can be seen enjoying the swings, as she tries to reclaim the phase of her lost childhood. Nearby there is an island called Mindanao where children can be seeing working on fields amid the agro decline. They had migrated from a place they refer to as "The Mountain of exhaustion" because, after centuries of mining it is very difficult to find gold there. But still, the exploration is going on. Some children instead of looking for gold, scavenge the mines for mercury spilled during the purification of gold, and Geneito is one of them. They hardly care about the poisonous and rotting effects of mercury. Some child miners still hammer the rock for almost 12 hours a day and in the evening miner emerge from the tunnels of the mountain of exhaustion to watch girls emerge into their adolescence in a nearby club. These Philipino girls usually below 18, come there to entertain and to sell their bodies.

In a nearby city of Manila, there lives a girl named Masarda, who was lured by the agents of an employment agency. The recruiter said that Manila was a nice place that offers good jobs and salaries. But later the employment agency would not release her and demanded 3000 Pesos. She was reduced into a piece of bone and skin. She reveals slave-like conditions in the bleaching industry. We ate like dogs and our food was rotten. But then luck came, UNICEF officials raided the place and they were rescued. Masarda is back in her home and she can be seen singing a popular song, "bitten by the lure of the city".

**Philosophical underline**

There are numerous disbeliefs about child labour, which justify the existence and perpetuation of the problem of child labour. The first disbelief is that employers are obliging children by employing them. But that is not the case. Employers are only concerned about their profits. Children can be exploited at no or very low cost. Second, Poverty is the single major cause of child labour. But the problem is much deeper. Poverty may be attributed to poor health, poor skills, lack of education and malnutrition. So these underlying problems have to be addressed. The third belief is that if children don't work, they and their families will starve. There is not always a direct correlation. Starvation is due to price policy, low income, and low purchasing power, income disparity, unequal food distribution, and unequal land ownership pattern. Fourthly, there is a belief that child labour is the result of the poor having more children. But the truth is that even children in small families are engaged in economic activities. There is child labour, not because of more children but because the families are denied their basic rights. Fifthly, there is a perception that work, equips children with skills for the future. But the reality is that tasks allotted to children are simple and repetitive. Skill is just a misnomer when applied to the backbreaking toil that children are engaged in. Rather hard physical labour, exposure to poisonous elements early in life damages the health of children. Sixthly, some say that child labour is necessary to preserve traditional art and craft. But learning a particular art craft by children should be integrated with education. It should not become an excuse of making money by employing children. Seventh is a wider perception that child labour cannot be abolished. But if we focus on every underlying issue and we complement them with a strong enforcement mechanism and strong will power then it is possible (next chapter on best practices are live examples).

# ANALYZING THE CASE STUDIES

# XXVII

# CAUSES OF CHILD LABOUR

After studying these case studies we can divide the cause into two categories: Demand and Supply.

**Demand side factors**: The demand side determinants are those which induce the employers to employ children

- Proliferation of informal sector.
- Employers prefer children as they constitute cheap labour
- Poor enforcement of legal provisions in the context of child labour (Almost in every case studied, the nation had anti-child labour law but the problem was with enforcement).
- Lack of strong determination and willpower among Government officials.
- Globalization, to an extent, has also given a boost to child labour. For example, demand for cocoa in Europe; the associated supply chain, and pieces of evidence of child labour seen in Ivory Coast.
- Creation of cultural myths by employers.

**Supply-side factors**: The supply-side determinants are those which make the parents or household head decide to utilize children's time as child labour.

- Families living in poverty.
- Parents, many a times do not get minimum wages.

- Large family size, as children are used as a means of income.
- Adult unemployment, under-employment, etc
- There is a lack of resources for survival and livelihood and therefore, families are forced to migrate in search of employment.
- Lack of basic services like early childhood care facilities, primary health care, etc.
- Illiteracy of parents and hence parents are ignorant about the adverse consequences of child labour
- Absence of universal primary education and non-availability/ accessibility of schools.
- Tolerance of Child labour and lack of social apathy.
- There is a tradition among many families, of making children learn the family skill.
- Then patriarchal attitude i.e. attitude towards the girl where girls are meant to start working at an early age.

**Detailed analysis about causes behind child labour**

Why do the children work? In answering this question it should be noted that children do not normally choose to work. The decision of whether a child will work or go to school is generally taken by parents. In some very exceptional cases-such as children who were abducted, lost, or separated from their family of origin because of war or of some natural disasters-children themselves choose to work (Cigno, Rosati and Tzannatos, 2001).

All these determinants are discussed below.

**Poverty**: There exists controversy about the poverty-child labour nexus. Many researchers such as Grootaert & Kanbur (1995), Amin, Quayes and Rives (2004), Ranjan (2001), Rogers and Swinnerton (2004), and Rahman(1999) note that poverty is the main cause of child labour. In most cases, parents are forced to send their children to work just for mere survival.However, some studies such as Bhalotra and Heady (2003), Canagarajah and Nielsen (1999) failed to find an inverse relationship between child labour and household income. Khanam and Rahman (2008) analyzed the poverty hypothesis drawing macro and micro-level evidences. The economic development of a country reduces the incidence of child labour. Countries with very low per capita income, such as Sub-Saharan African countries, are experiencing a high incidence of child labour. The negative impact of economic growth on child labour has also been documented in some country region-specific studies such as Dessy and

Knowles (2001) for Latin America, Basu and Tzannatos (2003) forChina, Tzannatos (2003) for Thailand and Edmonds (2001) for Victnam.

At micro level, household decision-making theory explains that child labour exists because of the unbearable situation of a household. Non-work of children in an extremely poor household is considered as a 'luxury good' that a family cannot afford. If the adult income is below a certain threshold level, a household will send its children to work. The study of Hazan and Berdugo (2002) also confirms that child labour is a consequence of poverty. Tzannatos (2003) mentions that intergeneration transmission of child labour, is also widely observed.

That is, if parents are silk workers, it is most likely that their children will go for silk work rather than going to school. Under this situation, poverty may not play a major role.

**Vulnerability of household**: Anker (2000), Khan (2003) notes that child labour is prevalent in the most vulnerable families, as these families, because of very low income, cannot cope with the injury or illness of an adult member, disability or death of any parent, unemployment of adult member. Distress and disruption resulting from abandonment or divorce also force the children to work.

**Unequal distribution of income/resources**: Child labour is positively related to higher unequal distribution of income and resources (UNICEF, 1997; Ranjan 2001). Saeed (2000) and Hussain (1985) also confirmed this finding for Pakistan.

**Child's behavior and schooling performance**: This factor also influences the parental decision concerning child labour. If a child does not like school and/or brings poor results, parents are more likely to put him/her at work rather than at school.

**Child's nutrition and health**: Poor health condition of the children contributes to child labour positively. The malnourished children suffer from learning difficulties, and the dropout rate is quite high. These dropout children are absorbed by child labour force (Chaudhry and Hamid 1999; Khan, 2003).

**Credit market constraints**: Capital market failure also results in child labour. If households cannot meet educational expenses and are unable to borrow to this end, they send their children to work (Ranjan 2001; Fallon and Tzannatos 1998).

**Parents' education:** Parents' education plays an important role in whether a child will go to school or work. The Majority of child labourers belong to illiterate families (Khan 2001). Educated parents are aware of the worth of educating their children; illiterate parents consider schooling as wastage of time and money. So there is an inverse relationship between parents‘ education and the supply of child labour. Parent's education particularly mothers' education is vital to keep a child in school.

**Family size and birth order**: Statistics show that the bigger the family size, the greater the likelihood that the children will work rather than attend school (Khan, 2003). This is because families with a large number of children cannot afford the schooling costs of all the children, so some children start working to support themselves and their school-going siblings. Khanam and Rahman (2007, 2008) note that older children are more likely to be sent to work than their younger siblings though a few exceptions also exist in the literature. The reasons may be mentioned that earlier-born children could be more productive to command higher wages or be more able to do household work or farming activities because of their higher innate abilities. This may induce parents to choose their older children for work. Further, as young family earners, parents may not have sufficient income to send their earlier born to school, as the earning schedule goes up with age.

Among the other determinants, unaffordable schooling costs, unavailability of quality education, availability of work for children, employer's attitudes, demand in the family business, remoteness, and inappropriate government policy contribute to the issue of child labour. Most of the population in developing countries live in rural areas where child labour is more prevalent because of traditional social and cultural norms that easily accept child labour (Neumayer and De Soysa 2005 quoted from Edmonds & Pavcnik 2002 and López-Calva, 2001).

# XXVIII

# TYPES OF CHILD LABOUR

- **Invisible child labour:** This includes children working in unorganized or informal sectors and very often they don't come under the purview of the law. Moreover, they constitute a substantial proportion of labour in the country. They may be working in agricultural fields or small factories.
- **Migrant Child labour:** Some children migrate from rural to urban areas or from smaller to larger towns/cities, either with families or alone. They migrate either for better employment opportunities or to escape from bondage.
- **Bonded Child labour**: Children are pledged by their parents/ guardians to employers instead of debt payments. The rate of interest on loans is so high that the amount to be repaid accumulates every year, making repayment almost impossible.
- **Children on streets**: They include working children who have families but spend most of their time on the streets. They usually earn for themselves and may or may not contribute to the family income.
- **Children off the streets:** Working childrenwho have left their families in villages or towns and have migrated to the city. They don't have a place to live in and hence, spend their nights at the railway platforms, bus stations, etc.
- **Abandoned or orphaned children:** Working children without families or whose families have abandoned them. They spend their lives on the streets without any kind of support and hence are the most exploited and

abused amongst the lot.

- **Abducted children:** Acase as seen in war-stricken African countries. Children are abducted during the conflict and are coercively made to work. Moreover, some mafias operate by kidnapping children, who are trafficked and are made to labour hard.
- **Domestic labour:** It is a very common form of child labour. Domestic work is performed by children below the relevant minimum age. Some people prefer children because they are easy to mold and work for longer hours for less wages.

# XXIX

# CONSEQUENCES: INFERENCES FROM CASE STUDIES

Child labour is considered an epidemic in the global economy and society. It has many undesirable effects concerning children's education, mental and physical development. Immature and inexperienced child labourers probably never realize the short and long terms' risks associated with their work. Their work steals their childhood.

Sometimes child labourers work for a long time and are very often denied a basic school education, normal playtime, social interaction, personal development, love and emotional support from their family. The society and economy as a whole are also affected because of child labour.

Some important consequences are noted below.

**Damaged physical development**: Child labour adversely affects physical, mental and social development of children. Because of poverty they are already suffering from malnutrition. With this physical weakness, if they do physically strenuous activities, this may lead to stunted growth. Child labourers tend to be shorter and lighter than non-working children. This growth deficiency also impacts their adult life. Because of accidents at work, some children have even lost their vital organs and thus been handicapped for the rest of their lives. BBS (2003) reports that out of 7.4 million working children about 0.6 million or 7.6 percent got hurt or sick due to their work in Bangladesh. Some children even die. In Bangladesh, ten children earning around $11 per month got burnt to death in a garment factory in November 2000.

Because children differ from adults in their physiological and psychological make-up, they are more susceptible to and are more adversely affected by specific work hazards than adults. Not yet matured mentally, they are less aware of the potential risks involved in the workplace. The effects of hazardous working conditions on children's health and development can be devastating. The impact of physically strenuous work, such as carrying heavy loads or being forced to adopt unnatural positions at work, can permanently distort or disable growing bodies. There is evidence that children are more vulnerable than adults to chemical hazards and that they have much less resistance to diseases. The hazards and risks to health may also be compounded by the lack of access to health facilities and education, poor housing and sanitation, and inadequate diet.

**Hinders mental or social development**: Also very often children are abused in their workplaces which makes them emotionally weak. As they do not have sufficient time to play with peers, proper socialization is lacking; lack of education hampers intellectual and mental development. Their self-esteem and required activities are always compromised which very often leads them to live in poverty (ICCLE, 2005). Children are much more vulnerable than adults to physical, sexual, and emotional abuse and suffer worse psychological damage in form of being denigrated, humiliated, or oppressed from working in environments that are exploitative, dangerous, and isolating. Children who suffer ill-treatment, abuse, and neglect at the hands of their employers may, as a consequence, find it very difficult to form attachments with and have feelings for others. They may have problems interacting and cooperating with others; in attaining a real sense of identity and belonging. They often lack confidence and have low self-esteem. These vulnerabilities are particularly true for the very young and girls.

**Intergenerational poverty**: Child labour continues the inter-generational poverty. It is observed that the parents of child labourers were child labourers themselves; they grew up as semi-skilled, illiterate or semi-illiterate, unemployed or underemployed adults. They are poor, and their poverty forced them to send their children to work prematurely which jeopardizes the future of their children to grow up as an educated and skilled person.

**Effects on educational achievement**: Child work adversely affects children's educational achievements at school. The children who work and attend school are generally observed with lower attendance rates and poor academic performance. BBS (2003) reports that 2.5 percent of child labourers attend school in Bangladesh, of which 68.3 percent noted that their work affects their regular school attendance and studies. The literacy rate of the non-child labourers was significantly higher than that of child labourers (62.1 percent versus 52.1 percent). The study of Heady (2000) on Ghana also revealed that child work had a substantial negative effect on learning achievement in the key areas of reading and mathematics. This may be because of, as the author mentioned, exhaustion or because of a diversion of interest away from academic concerns. They do not obtain the basic level of education that is needed to cope in life. When these activities are abandoned in favor of work, children are pushed into adulthood before they are ready.

**Adult unemployment and reduced bargaining power**: Employers prefer to hire children as a cheap source of labour, and children are easy to manage because they are more obedient and are less aware of their rights than adults. Children are hardly protected against the employer's decisions concerning wages, working hours and work environment. As children substitute some of the adults' work, adult unemployment increases; this in turn, reduces the ability of adults to bargain for fair wages. As a result, the overall wage rate decreases. In the literature, parallel growth of child labour and adult unemployment is evident. For example, in October 2004, the number of unemployed persons in the Philippines was recorded at 3.9 million, and the number of working children was also nearly 4 million. This reflects that there is a close correlation between the prevalence of child labour and adult unemployment (ICCLE, 2005).

**Children and household well-being**: It is argued that some positive benefits of child labour may also be realized. Child labourers can gain some human capital from their workplace experience such as vocational training, learning by doing, the potential for making contacts, learning job market strategies, etc. Sometimes, child labour is the only way to finance a child's education, which, in turn, could bring better outcomes for the younger children (Emerson and Souza, 2007; Horn 1994; Akabayashi and Psacharopoulos, 1999).

Child labour has also an effect on household well-being. For example, BBS (2003) reported that 68.9 percent of parents in Bangladesh opined that the living standard of their household would decrease if the children stop working. About 7.9 percent of parents in rural areas expressed their concern that it would be difficult for them to survive if their children stop working. About 2.6 percent of parents in urban areas and 2.4 percent of parents in rural areas pointed out that unless their children did not work, it would be difficult for them to run family businesses.

# BEST PRACTICES: MACRO LEVEL

# XXX

# PENCIL PORTAL

The PENCIL Portal (India) is an integrated application system that is based on the technology that primarily aims at the submission of complaints by any citizens of the country from anywhere and anytime basis for the easy communication between the nodal officers of the Government departments and also enables the citizens to track the status of the registered complaints.

- It mandates a uniform and systematic approach towards the monitoring of the process by adopting a general classification and standardization of filing complaints and eases the efforts across the Government departments.
- This portal facilitates the online lodging of complaints that are registered by the general citizens to the concerned Departments, Ministries and Organizations which can be linked to their official portal.
- The PENCIL portal facilitates the monitoring of complaints and reports as per the requirements of Government departments for the effective monitoring of the pending reports.
- It facilitates the user with the generation of automated notifications such as Acknowledgement and replies for the official correspondence with the complainants.
- This application is most flexible to be extended as per the requirements of Government departments for quick and effective action for the registered complaints that are found to be genuine.
- All the complaints filed by the citizen gets assigned automatically by the system to the respective Nodal Officer for the rescue,

rehabilitation and mainstreaming of the child labourer.
- Successful mainstreaming into legal schools of all children who have been withdrawn from child labour and rehabilitated through the National Child labour Protection scheme.

**Components under PENCIL Portal**

The below following are the various components of PENCIL Portal that are namely:

- Child Tracking System
- Complaint Corner
- State Government
- National Child Labour Project and
- Convergence.

**Implementation Process**

All complaints filed will be received by the District Nodal Officers (DNOs) who are nominated by the Districts. After receiving the complaints, the rescue measures will be taken within the time frame of 48 hours in coordination with the police.

# XXXI

# NATIONAL CHILD LABOUR PROJECT: INDIA

National Child Labour Project is the Indian Government Scheme which has been devised to tackle the issue of child labor in a more effective manner by focusing on specific target ideas, identifying the victims, withdrawing them from hazardous situations, focusing on their rehabilitation and meanwhile spreading awareness on the functionalities of NCLP and the other agencies on child labour to the families of the child labourers.

## ***Objectives of NCLP:***

It aims at the expulsion of child labour in all forms possible through a sequential basis of:

- Identification of children in child labour in the project area.
    - Withdrawing the identified children.
    - Preparation of the withdrawn children for introduction to mainstream education by providing necessary vocational training.
    - Ensuring that they're benefitted from the multitude of services provided by the different governments and agencies.

It aims at the withdrawal of adolescent children from hazardous situations or occupations by:

- Identifying all adolescents and withdrawing them from the project area.
- Facilitating training programmes for such adolescents through the skill development schemes which currently exist.
- It aims at raising awareness amongst the target communities and the other stakeholders regarding child labour about the functionality of NCLP.
- To create a Child Labour Monitoring, tracking and Reporting System to stay updated with the situation.

## ***NCLP Target Group:***

- The scheme focuses on all the child workers below the age of 14 in the target areas, adolescent workers below 18 years of age engaged in hazardous occupations and also on the families of the child workers in that specific target areas.
- The children would be eased into local schools after providing necessary bridging programmes.
- The adolescent children in hazardous work would be given skill enhancement training and be shifted to non-hazardous work.
- The delivery of income/stipend, employment or social security to the families of child workers will be ensured by the government. The tracking of the rescued child workers will be done to follow up for evaluation of impact.
- The child labour laws will be stepped up according to the requirement.

## ***NCLP Highlights/Features:***

- The Government contributes to the identification, classification, eradication, and withdrawal of children and adolescents from hazardous occupations.

- Successfully mainstreaming the rescued children into proper local schools and affiliating them with Sarva Shiksha Abhiyan (SSA).
- The adolescents will be provided with other skill enhancement trainings and shall be transferred to permitted occupations.
- Better awareness programs for the education of communities and the Indian public as a whole with the help of enhanced abilities.
- Compensatory measures for the families who are releasing their children from working and allowing them to attend training or schools.
- Mothers of such victimized children are often organized into Self-help groups (SHG's).

## ***NCLP Implementation:***

- The scheme was successfully implemented through joint collaboration with civil society, state and district administration.
- The responsibility is jointly handed to the respective state governments and the Ministry of Labour and Employment.
- The scheme has been initially launched in areas of high cases of child labour and specific District Project Societies (DPS's) have been set up at the district level to ensure proper implementation of the scheme at all levels.
- District Project Society is also responsible for the stipend payment for the children and their families.

# XXXII

# SOCIAL PHOTOGRAPHY MODEL: AMERICA

In 1890, nearly 1.5 million children aged between 10 and 15 were employed in U.S.A. and in 1900, nearly 16% of workers were under the age of 16. They were employed in the factory mines, and cotton mills. They were less likely to unionize; easier to control; could be offered lower wages; could work longer hours and were feasible for smaller machines.

After 2 boys at Chaucel Collery (West Nanticoke) were suffocated to death and after a 15-year-old boy named Arthur Albecker, had both his legs crushed at his workplace, National Child labour committee was formed in 1904. Its member Florence Kelly one remarked:

"Never again can it be a matter of mere concern what hours the children are working. They will be the Republic when we are dead; and we cannot leave it to the local legislators, here and there, to decide unobserved what sort of citizens shall be produced in this or that state, whether they shall be strong in body, mind and character, or whether they shall grow up enfeebled by overwork in early childhood"

John Spargo wrote in his article with a title "Bitter cry of Children", 1906

"I once stood in a breaker for half an hour and tried to do that work which a 12-year-old boy was doing day after day, for 10 hours at a stretch, for sixty cents a day. The gloom of the breaker appalled me. Outside the sun shone brightly, the air was pellucid, and the birds sang in chorus with trees and rivers. Within the breaker there was blackness, clouds of deadly dust enfolding everything, the harsh, the grinding roar of machinery and the ceaseless rushing of coal through chutes, filled the ears. I tried to pick out the pieces of slate from the hurrying streams of coal, often missing them; my hands were bruised and cut in a few minutes, I was covered from head to foot with coal dust, and for many hours I was expectorating some of the small particles of anthracite I had swallowed."

**Social photography campaign**

Lewis Hine was hired in 1907 by the National Child Labour committee who taught sociology at New York City's Ethical Culture School. He used photography as a means of social change. His ideas were to gather data and evidence which would form the basis of sending petitions to state legislatures to pass "minimum age" laws, to stop child labour. He photographed immigrants arriving at Ellis Island and the coal mines in Pennsylvania where adolescent breaker boys were removing impurities from coal. Similarly, he photographed Sardine cutters in Maine; Oyster workers in Louisiana as young as 4; Tobacco pickers in Kentucky; Cranberry pickers in Massachusetts, etc.

When not allowed to enter the factory premise, he would wait outside factories and would click the photos of child labourers standing near windows; entering the door, etc. He would write a detailed caption below the photographs mentioning wages, work conditions and would also show horrific injuries. There were some interesting posters with titles like "Making Human Junk"; "Shall we let industry shackle the nation"; "Everybody pays but few profit by child labour" etc. He coined the term photo stories and his photos usually humanized the life photos, to the otherwise indifferent public. There were some unique features of his photography. There was a shallow depth in his photographic field; he would emphasize the workers and not machinery and clicks were usually at eye level. All this gave a humanistic touch and aroused a feeling of pity and empathy for the children at work

**Subsequent events**

The Keating-Owen Act was passed by the Federal legislature which banned the sale of products from any factory and shop that employed children under 14 but the law was declared unconstitutional by Supreme Court. Similarly, the Revenue Act, placed a Federal tax of 10% on all goods produced with the use of child labour but again it was declared unconstitutional. Subsequently, the Child labour Amendment Act 1924 was passed but it was not ratified by the states. Finally, after the great depression, serious efforts were made to tackle child labour because child laborers were posing huge competition to the adult workers, who were already struggling for survival after the Wall Street crash.

# XXXIII

# BOLSA FAMILIA: BRAZIL

Bolsa Familia is a Brazilian conditional direct cash transfer program aimed at households with family incomes equal to or less than a specified line for extreme poverty, provided they have children or adolescents from 0 to 17 years old. It provides financial aid to poor Brazilian families. If the families have children, they must ensure that the children attend school and are vaccinated.

These cash transfers play a dual role: on one hand by encouraging consumption they play a reactivating role in the economy, on the other hand, by making cash transfers contingent upon their children attending schools, the dropout rate of their children due to economic difficulties can be avoided.

Therefore, the program attempts to both *reduce short-term poverty* by direct cash transfers and fight *long-term poverty* by increasing human capital among the poor through conditional cash transfers. It also works to give free education to children who cannot afford to go to school, to show the importance of education. The Bolsa Familia program has also been mentioned as one factor contributing to the reduction of poverty in Brazil. The programme has also improved the job market in the country and minimum wages too have increased.

The programme works in **three dimensions** and aims to reduce the reproductive cycle of poverty and hence the child labour.

**Promote immediate poverty relief through direct cash transfers to families** :

Benefits are paid by the Federal Government directly to families, who withdraw the money each month from a banking network by the means of a magnetic card. Benefits are the sum total of three components: First, Basic Benefit (R$ 62): paid to families with monthly income per person up to R$ 69, irrespective of the number of children, adolescents, or youth. Second, Variable benefit (R$ 20): paid to families with monthly income per person up to R$ 137, per child or adolescent up to 15 years of age (maximum 3 benefits per family). Third, Variable youth benefit: paid to programme families with teenagers aged 16-17 who are studying (R$ 60; maximum two benefits per family).

**Strengthen the exercise of basic social rights** in the areas of healthcare, education and social assistance, through the fulfillment of conditionalities.

**Promote opportunities for the development of families**, through actions that promote the overcoming of vulnerability and poverty by BFP beneficiaries.

In summation, variable benefits according to the family composition that prioritizes children and adolescents, direct payment through a bank card, access to the program through a unified mechanism (*Cadastro Unico*), shared management responsibilities with states and municipalities, administration of quotas by municipality using an estimate of poor families developed in partnership with Brazilian Institute of Geography and Statistics.

**Requirements**

Beneficiaries are selected through a database for a unified register (Cadastro Único para Programas Sociales) which serves to assess the socioeconomic profiles and social needs of beneficiaries. In addition to being in poverty, families participating in the Bolsa Família Programme, must fulfill programme conditions in the areas of health and education. These conditions include keeping school-age children in school and complying with basic health care requirements, such as keeping the inoculation schedules for children, and attending medical appointments for pregnant women and nursing mothers. The object of the foregoing conditions is not to punish families but to lay responsibility jointly on beneficiaries and the public authorities, the latter being bound to identify the reasons for possible non-compliance with conditions and subsequently implement public policies to assist such families. The programme thus emphasizes the guarantee of the rights of persons. Compliance with requirements is monitored by the Ministries of Social Development,

Education, and Health, in coordination with local authorities. In the event of non compliance with the rules, families ***receive a notice*** with no penalty, and benefits continue. Upon the ***second notice***, the benefit is blocked for a period of 30 days and maybe unblocked if the case returns to normal. The ***third notice*** causes suspension of benefits for 60 days. With the ***last notice***, benefits are cancelled and the family is removed from the programme. In 2007 there were 1.5 million cases of non-compliance or 14% of all beneficiaries. Benefits were cancelled in only 34,050 cases (2%).

Assessments of the Bolsa Família Programme show that it had an immediate and significant effect on the living conditions of poor people as it helps to promote food and nutritional safety, reduce poverty and inequality, lower the risk of child labour, dynamize local economies, and promote gender equality. In addition, studies show that the program does not impede the incentive to work; on the contrary, the benefit has increased participation of men and women beneficiaries in the labour market, helping to reduce marginalization among many poor families.

# XXXIV

# The IPEC Project

The International Programme on Elimination of Child Labour is a global programme launched by the ILO, 1991. The long-term objective of IPEC is to contribute to the effective abolition of child labour. Its immediate objectives are:

- Enhancing the capacity of ILO constituents and Non Governmental Organizations to design, implement and evaluate programmes for Child Labour elimination.
- To identify interventions at community levels that could he serve as models for replication
- Creation of awareness and social mobilization for securing the elimination of child labour

At the international level, IPEC has a Programme Steering Committee consisting of representatives of ILO, donors, and participating countries. At the national level, there are

Steering Committees(which are tripartite in their composition), with representations from NGOs as well. IPEC works between the National Ministries of labour, the agencies receiving assistance and the ILO headquarters.

Two pillar approach of ILO/IPEC approach in its direct programmes have been:

- The economic empowerment of the household at risk
- Making education accessible and meaningful to the children concerned.

The ILO/IPEC approach is defined by

- Enrollment in elementary education for target group children aged 5-8 years
- Withdrawal through enforcement of labour laws

- The transition education for children between 9-13 years.
- Strengthened vocational training for children in the age group 14-17 years.
- Local community institution-building through thrift and credit management and enhancing women's socio- economic status.
- Strengthening public education through support for quality improvement.
- Social mobilization includes both community mobilization as well as a partnership of social actors such as trade unions and employers through tripartite partnerships.

# XXXV

# INDUS CHILD LABOUR PROJECT

It is a joint collaboration of USDOL (U.S. Department of Labour), the Indian Ministry of Labour and the ILO. It aims to eliminate child labour in selected hazardous sectors. The project recognizes that working children belong to specific sections of the population that continue to be marginalized. Therefore, it is the goal of the project to target marginalized populations of children in selected districts of India and to improve their attendance, performance, and retention in education.

Key strategies of the programme:

- **Enrolment in public elementary education**: Education as an alternative to child labour is now accepted as a well established strategy. It is in this context that the programme targets a large proportion of young children (5-8 years) for enrollment in elementary education. The idea is that the progressive elimination of child labour is directly linked to full enrollment and retention of children in the formal education system.
- **Provision of transitional education**: Transitional education has been seen to have the potential to play a catalytic role in transforming the attitude of children who have dropped out of the formal education system. Recognizing, the special needs of older working children (9-13 years), the programme focuses on providing a bridge course to enable a smooth transition to mainstream, either formal education or vocational training.

- **Strengthening vocational training**: The objective of the project is to present demonstrable models for withdrawal of child labour, it places special emphasis on providing skill training to the older child and adolescent workers (14-17 years). The training will be provided for 1 year at a pre-identified training institute. The curriculum for vocational training will include practical training, basic literacy, numeracy, and life skill education. Each target area will assess the labour market needs and demands before the identification of the training curriculum. Efforts will be made to either complement the existing trade skills or to introduce allied marketable skills and forge linkages with employers.
- **Local community institution building**: Recognizing the significant contribution that parents of rehabilitated child labour can offer in transforming the attitude of the family and community towards child labour, the programme specifically targets mothers of children enrolled in Technical pre vocational educational centers through the formation of viable Self-help groups. To compensate for the real and imagined loss of income, in releasing the children to participate in the formal education system, efforts will be made to organize mothers of child laborers into SHGs and they will also be encouraged to avail short-term vocational skill training programmes at the I.T.I.'s.
- **Strengthening public education of child labourers**: Quality elementary education is extremely important for prevention of child labour. Financial compulsions often leave children with little alternative but to enter the labour market. While primary education is free in India, child labour families perceive an opportunity cost to educate their children. Therefore the project recognizes the need to strengthen education infrastructure in the country.
- **Social Mobilization:** To mobilize the considerable existing resources of civil society for the cause, and to help make the general public aware of the problem of child labour and its negative consequences.

**Dimensions in the implementation of the project**

- The existence of an efficient and sustainable monitoring system for the ground-level child labour situation.
- To determine the extent to which child labour is prevalent.

In this context an effective child labour monitoring system is needed which should:

- Ensure that workplaces are free from child labour and that various social protection measures benefit children and their families
- Mobilize government officials and civil society members to guard against the continuance and emergence of new children labour and hazardous child labour sectors
- Verify continuously that children are not at a risk of getting into either child labour or hazardous child labour
- Verify that children are working acceptably: Children below 14 are not employed and those above 15 years are not in hazardous labour
- Ensure improved working conditions, especially with respect to healthier working conditions and implementation of core labour standards.

**Beneficiaries**

- Identified young child workers (5-8 years) who will be directly enrolled in regular schools.
- Old child workers (9-13 years), who will be provided with transitional education and support services.
- Adolescent workers (14-17 years), who will be provided with vocational training.
- Parents of working children will be organized into self-help groups and later provided with skills for additional income generation.

The following sectors were identified as priority areas for action under the project: hand-rolled cigarettes, brassware, handmade bricks, Fireworks, footwear, Hand blown glass bangles, handmade locks, etc

# XXXVI

# HARVEST GARDEN MODEL: ARGENTINA

Tobacco is widely grown in the fields of Salta, South Argentina. Numerous children used to work on the fields; in curing centers and associated activities like drying the tobacco leaves, hand dropping the tobacco leaves over the processing belts. The working conditions were not good; children were missing out on education, but then some interesting steps were taken.

Tobacco Producers cooperatives, Tobacco chamber of Salta, and ILO joined hands to establish "Harvest gardens". It is a unique concept in which employers, worker organizations and government share responsibilities to eradicate the menace of child labour. They tried to build children's self-esteem through various strategies. Just close to the plantations, these places ensured education to the children of plantation workers, and sports were promoted too. Children are holistically taken care of while their parents work on the plantations. Simultaneously there was a dedicated campaign to enhance social security measures of the families and local administration took a special onus in the documentation work.

There is a special thrust towards using machines but to that extent which doesn't displace the adult laborers. Simultaneously there is a concept of "NETWORK" which is a P.P.P. model between government and 90 private companies. There is a joint pact to eliminate child labour from agro fields and at workplaces in the supply chain.

Ministry of Labour is working closely with other ministries for giving special focus on the child labourers to ensure quality education, healthcare and vocational skills within these harvest gardens and also in local schools.

ILO gives technical assistance; guides the employers; has created training modules for adolescent child labourers. Simultaneously a frequent tripartite social dialogue (amongst employers, workers, and government officials) is promoted at a local level to ensure collective problem solving and decision making. Not only this, there is often an involvement of trade unions in this dialogue.

Lastly, techno-advancements are jointly focused upon: Advanced chambers have removed the need of hand dropping of tobacco leaves on canes by children and modern curing centers are being used to dry the tobacco.

# BEST PRACTICES: MICRO LEVEL

# XXXVII
# AL-TAHRIR PROJECT: IRAQ

Child labour is quite prevalent in Iraq. Children can be seen working in houses, workshops, industries, and streets, where they suffer abuse in many forms: verbal, physical, and sexual.

But Al-Tahrir association for development, an NGO came forward and established five psycho-social support centers. These centers partnered with local authorities to ensure an integrated and sustainable response. Simultaneously community policing in Ninawa had become quite active and there was a strong linkage between citizens and social services.

Moreover, with the support and collaboration of ILO, there is a programme to support children; provide employment opportunities to the families; spread awareness on negative aspects of this phenomenon. A unique feature is that *daily they collect information*, regarding working children on streets, at the traffic light; in the market area, and other workplaces that have a high prevalence of child labour.

A spokesperson said:

“We register the cases in databases and we have interesting activities in our centers, which we divide among the rescued children like computing, music, drama, and art. We also have psychotherapists which provide counseling to these kids who might have gone through a different form of abuse and they try to redeem the self-esteem of the kid. Therefore we support them both mentally and socially”

# XXXVIII

# ARISE PROJECT: ZAMBIA

Like in many African countries, child labour is a grim menace in the nation. Children can be seen collecting pieces of charcoal; working in tobacco plantations; picking up caterpillars out of the trees and then cooking them in dried sand; carrying heavy cans of water in tobacco nurseries among many other places where they can be seen working.

ILO has partnered with Zambian authorities to come up with ARISE project. It is also a PPP project whereby local district child labour committees follow an integrated approach:

- Awareness generation in collaboration with local NGOs. Community theatres and musical events in schools are designed to point out dangers.
- Identifying child laborers via inspections.
- Special education modules for rescued children.
- Youth resource centers have been established whereby adolescents are provided training as part of apprenticeship programmes. For example, In Kaoma-Nikegyamo city they are trained to manage fish, chicken, and meat farms. A regional approach is followed and they are also trained in masonry, carpentry, etc

SHGs are promoted amongst vulnerable families and there is a guided bank linking with SHGs.

# XXXIX

# VELPUR VILLAGE MODEL: INDIA

Velpur, a progressive agriculture village in Armoor sub-division(Telangana, India) stands out for making the mandal child labour-free. All the 8057 children in the mandal were in schools. The village community played a key role. All gram panchayats passed formal resolutions banning child labour in all forms and undertook to send all children to schools. They decided to ostracize anybody who employs a child for work. This included the 800 plus children brought back to schools and the nine mentally retarded children identified during the drive and admitted to an institution catering to them.

The villagers not only wrote off almost 37 lakh, which were taken as loans keeping these children as a guarantee (and was due from their parents) but also provided books and dresses for these children to join the schools. About 1400 girls were studying in the 34 non-residential bridge schools of the project in the district in 2001.

Mr. Asok Kumar (district collector) said, "The close monitoring and daily feedback by the team in the field helped in making course corrections and changing strategies suited to various situations arising in the field on a day-to-day basis. These efforts culminated in making Velpur a child labor free mandal—having all 5-15-year-old children in schools", he said with a sense of satisfaction.

# XL

# SOLUTIONS

**Broader ideas**

- Developing a multi-stakeholder process through transformative agenda at international, national, and local levels. At each level, there should be "mechanisms for vertical and horizontal communications, joint planning and coordinated implementation of synergistic actions". Plans should also be developed to address all the root causes of gaps to eliminate child labour.
- To create a systems approach, adopted with a continual improvement of initiatives based on consistent feedback from quantitative and qualitative data collected on child labour elimination initiative and child labour prevalence.
- A result-based management system be developed and implemented, building on, and expanding due diligence accountability systems of all stakeholders.

**SOLUTIONS : As inferred from the above case studies**

- Child labour can be reduced through the economic security of children. When the issue of poverty is addressed, child labour can be tackled automatically.
- There is a need to check the unorganized labour market because almost all children are found in this sector.
- The goal of universalization of elementary education is not achieved yet and there should be more initiatives that need to be undertaken; the poor

people should be made aware of their rights, values, family planning and the value of their children.

- The law enforcement machinery should be made effective with efficient monitoring vigilant system to implement the legislative and constitutional provisions and administrative measures to ensure free and compulsory education for all children of this nation.
- Laws related to Child labourers should be transparent and easily understandable by a layman.
- There is no need for any new law to protect the rights of children but proper implementation of the present laws is required.
- Awareness should be created in the common masses through campaigns, seminars, etc.
- A special fund, be earmarked in all education budgets for such awareness campaigns.
- It is important to deal with those industries and employers strictly, who encourage child labour, and very importantly *certainty of punishment is required rather than the extremity of punishment.*
- Employment opportunities should be created for adults or parents of child labourers rather than focusing only on rescuing child labour. The rescue of child labourers can never be a final and lasting solution to the problem. *Rescuing child labourers from labour without economic security is worthless.*
- Basic facilities should be provided to the poor children as they are essential for their development.
- Governments across the world should arrange free medical checkups for poor children and child labourers who cannot afford the medical expenditure.
- All forms of mass media should disseminate information about all aspects of National minimum wages, in all languages, regularly to empower the labourers of the unorganized sector.
- Additional resources have to be generated to fulfill the target of compulsory education.
- India faces the problem of overpopulation which is related to child labour directly or indirectly. Therefore a vibrant policy to check population control is needed.
- Dissemination of information regarding children's rights as well as about existing laws, legal provisions, and support structure should be made obligatory.

- Parents should be informed about the rights of children through seminars, camps, workshops, etc.
- Collaboration with NGOs and voluntary organizations should be encouraged.
- Partnerships and initiatives of Governments and corporate actors should be aligned with international conventions, standards, guidelines, national policies, and plans. Also, there is a need of improving existing partnerships and cross-border agreements. In addition, agreements of initiatives for the identification, return and reintegration of trafficked children should be scaled up. And finally, it should be a priority to ensure that child labour elimination is directly cited and fully integrated into all economic development policies and plans, especially in agriculture-related economic activities or investments. Including in the design and monitoring of the plans.
- The E.U. Commission points out those social protection mechanisms to help protect environmental, health, social, and other shocks should be developed and expanded. In addition, local development plans should be adapted or developed to be more comprehensive, integrated, strengthened and synergistic concerning child labour protection systems. Among other recommendations, there should be an increased construction of physical infrastructure, with emphasis on roads, accessible schools, child protection infrastructure and one-stop referral locations for children in, or at risk, of child labour and other exploitation.

# BIBLIOGRAPHY


- **Newspapers**

  - The Hindu
  - Indian Express
  - The Tribune
  - Hindustan Times

- **Government Publications**

  - Census of India 2011
  - National human development Report, 2001
  - 66$^{th}$ Round of NSSO on survey

- **Websites**

  - www.ilo.org
  - www.childrerightsindia.org
  - www.humanism.org
  - www.indiatogether.org
  - www.jstor.org
  - www.ignited.in
  - www.researchgate.net

- **YouTube documentaries** : by UNICEF; VICE; Al-Jazeera; I.L.O, Jimmy-O-Donnel and CGTN Americas Now; Sky news and CBS mornings; Andreas Birch; Brethren voices; Journeyman pictures; Euronews; Channels Television; TRT world; DW News; Journeyman pictures ;Jibs bank; infoMigrants; Zak films; BBC News; Human Rights Watch; FAU research; CAN.

- **Other references**:

  - Sekar H.R.(2001), Child labour in Home based lock industry of Aligarh, VV Giri National Labour Institute Noida

- Ghosh, A. and Sekar,H.R.(2002), Child labour in the knife industry of Rampur, VV Giri National Labour Institute Noida
- Ghosh,R. and Sharma,R. (2003), Child Labour in glass bangle industry of Ferozabad, VV Giri National Labour Institute Noida
- Child labour in Brassware industry of Moradabad, Child labour series(1992, N.R.C. on Child labour, VV Giri National Labour Institute Noida
- Working children of the Pottery industry of Khurja. Child labour series(1992), VV Giri National Labour Institute Noida.
- Sekar, H.R.(2003), Child labour in hazardous industries: The slaughter house and allied occupations, , VV Giri National Labour Institute Noida.
- Sekar, H.R.(2003), Child labour in urban informal sector: A study of Rag pickers in Noida, VV Giri National Labour Institute Noida
- Sekar,H.R. (2007) Child Labour: Situation and strategies for Elimination, VV Giri National Labour Institute Noida.
- UNICF; 1997. The state of world children
- Pati, R.N.(1991), Rehabilitation of Child Labourers in India, Ashish Publications, New Delhi.
- Kaur, Sukhpal(2016), Problem of Child Labour in India.

www.ingramcontent.com/pod-product-compliance
Ingram Content Group UK Ltd.
Pitfield, Milton Keynes, MK11 3LW, UK
UKHW041852190726
13854UKWH00002B/856

9 798886 297430